LEGACY

Taking care of the most important people
in your life when you are no longer here

First published in 2021 by Melisa Sloan

A catalogue entry for this book is available from the National Library of Australia.

ISBN: 978-1-922553-05-8

Printed in Australia by McPherson's Printing
Project management and text design by Publish Central
Cover design by Peter Reardon

The paper this book is printed on is certified as environmentally friendly.

Disclaimer
The material in this publication is of the nature of general comment only, and does not represent professional advice. It is not intended to provide specific guidance for particular circumstances and it should not be relied on as the basis for any decision to take action or not take action on any matter which it covers. Readers should obtain professional advice where appropriate, before making any such decision. To the maximum extent permitted by law, the author and publisher disclaim all responsibility and liability to any person, arising directly or indirectly from any person taking or not taking action based on the information in this publication.

Contents

If you're going to live,
leave a legacy. Make a
mark on the world that
can't be erased.

Maya Angelou

Introduction

What will *your* legacy be?

You have worked hard for your wealth. You have sacrificed so many things to get where you are today, and quite likely at times operated on autopilot in your quest for success. You have given it your all, plus more.

Right now, the last thing you would want to happen is that all your hard work comes undone, all the long hours, the grind, the tears, and the triumphs.

This could happen though if you do not have the appropriate documentation in place to prepare for when you are no longer here.

So, I encourage you to think about one question…

WHAT WILL YOUR LEGACY BE?

Legacy means different things to different people, or it may mean nothing at all. To some it means building an extremely successful business, to others it is receiving accolades and having a stadium named after them, to others it may mean helping others and providing inspiration in how they live their daily lives.

To most people though, the most significant legacy you can leave is to look after your family. To show them that they mattered, that you cared and loved them enough to ensure you took the time to put your Estate Plan in place. An Estate Plan that comprises of the relevant documents, that clearly explains your wishes of what you would like to happen to your wealth when you are no longer here, to ensure that your loved ones are taken care of, to ensure that your wishes are clear, and to provide guidance and instructions in respect to what is to happen to your business interests and entities.

I am fortunate enough to wake up every day and do something that I love: helping people put their legacy in place. Sometimes it takes a few times to get all the pieces of the client's puzzle in the correct places, particularly if the client has complex asset and trust structures, however we persevere, and the end result is we collectively put a well-documented Estate Plan in place that is reflective of our client's wishes. It also provides our clients with much craved peace of mind, knowing that if they became incapacitated or died that everything will happen the way they want it to and that their family will be cared for.

DYING WITHOUT A WILL

Although I love what I do, like every job there are some not-so-good aspects, the 'ugly bits' I call them. Those ugly bits can revolve around the fact that almost fifty percent of Australian adults die without a Will. I personally find this figure astounding. It means that almost fifty percent of adults essentially do not take the time to put a Will in place that will take care of their family when they are gone.

As an estate planning and probate lawyer, I have extensive experience assisting grieving families to deal with the consequences of a loved one passing away without a Will and other estate planning documents in place. I can tell you, it is not pretty. Losing a loved one unexpectedly is horrific; there is the emotional trauma to deal with, the despair, the loss, the unexpected change to life, the family unit and financial circumstances.

When you die without a Will your estate is distributed in accordance with the intestacy provisions determined by the government. The intestacy provisions vary depending on your family circumstances, such as whether you are married, whether you have children from your current marriage and whether you have children from other relationships, or no spouse or no children at all.

As a result, dying without a Will may mean that your wife can no longer continue to live in the house that you had both happily lived in for the last twenty years, your forever home, because she needs to sell it so your children from your previous marriage can receive their entitlement to your estate. Is this really what you intended to happen when you were gone? Did you really think there would come a time where your wife may now have to rent a property because she can no longer afford to purchase a new home with her share of your estate?

What happens when you die without a Will?

If you die without a Will your next of kin will need to make an application to the relevant Court to become an administrator of your estate and there may be a few stumbling blocks along the way, including your next of kin may be directed by the Court to find guarantors to provide a guarantee of a specified sum to satisfy the Court until such time that the estate is paid to all beneficiaries in accordance with the intestacy provisions. Until such time that your next of kin is granted Letters of Administration, it can often be difficult for them to access the relevant information they require, taking up considerable time and causing much stress and emotional turmoil.

So why do so many Australian adults not put a Will in place?

There are several reasons people don't put their Will and Estate Plan in place; for many it is something that they are going to do 'one day'. For others they think that it is only something that you put in place when you are old, and some people have a phobia that if they put a Will in place that they shall die. Fact: a number of clients have made this comment to me and they are still very much alive, so fingers crossed they have overcome this phobia.

I once met a charming man; he was seventy-six and proudly told me that he didn't have a Will in place. When I enquired why, he very enthusiastically told me that both his parents had lived well into their nineties, so he was young by comparison and consequently had ample time to put his estate planning affairs into place. Let us hope he doesn't get hit by a bus any time soon.

Many people do not like talking about their mortality or what will happen when they are no longer here. They would rather plan a holiday, do gardening and catch up with family or friends. Anything to avoid the elephant in the room. There are many underlying emotions that relate to this topic that people put in the too-hard box and never address.

The underlying reasons many people do not put their legacy and Estate Plan in place are:

- they don't know where to start
- they don't make the time
- they are too busy creating a life to provide for their family
- they don't have their eyes on the final act
- they find it an overwhelming process with legal jargon that they don't understand.

But it doesn't have to be that way. It's my aim to make it an easier process for you, to educate you and support you along the way.

As an estate planning lawyer, I want to help all of those who don't know where to start. I want to help those who do not know how to navigate the elephant in the room. I want to help you put the best possible Estate Plan in place for your family. I want you to celebrate once you have done so because you are making a difference to the lives of those you love.

WHAT'S IN THIS BOOK?

This book has been written for you, for those of you who love and care for your family and loved ones and want to provide for them in the event that something happens to you, whether you become incapacitated or if you die. It's written to help you understand the important concepts of an Estate Plan, and to provide you with the tools to identify what you want to implement so that you can articulate your wishes clearly and concisely to those who can assist you in creating your legacy and putting your Estate Plan in place.

This book aims to be thought provoking, and will perhaps raise issues you had not previously considered. There is no sample family: all family units are different – you may be single, married, a blended family, have children who cannot control their inheritance, estranged children, or perhaps disabled children. You may have a wonderful business operation, or you may have several. In addition, you may control Trusts and have superannuation. All these aspects are carefully detailed in this book to provide you with answers to the most common questions people ask.

Essentially, this book should be utilised as a guide to work through the different components of an Estate Plan that are relevant to your individual circumstances. As such, given that you may not read every chapter of this book in methodical order, there are some points that are repeated throughout this book, to emphasise relevant points.

This book contains general advice only. Like all legal matters you should obtain legal advice specific to your own circumstances from an estate planning lawyer when creating your Estate Plan to enable it to be tailored to your specific needs and requirements. Reading this book should allow you to attend your initial consultation with your estate planning lawyer armed with all the information you have accumulated in reading this book and with definitive instructions of what you would like to put in place.

Why am I so passionate about you creating your legacy and Estate Plan? I have seen the alternative, I have seen the pain, stress, emotional toll, and once close families destroyed when someone dies without a Will. It could have all been avoided, so simply, if the deceased had taken the time to put their Estate Plan in place. I want to educate and encourage people to put their Estate Plans in place, I want to promote change so that the incomprehensible statistic of almost fifty percent of Australians dying without a Will is diminished as it will so greatly impact the lives of those left behind in a more positive way.

It is my wish that you, the reader, gain clarity, comfort, and reassurance in reading this book. That you are encouraged and empowered to create your legacy and take care of the people that matter the most in your life. You have worked hard to get this far, so why not make your ending your most significant act.

Putting an Estate Plan in place can be the greatest legacy that you leave behind when you are no longer here, and your family and loved ones will be eternally grateful that you took the time to put this in place, something so small but so beautifully touching to know they were loved.

We all die. The goal isn't to live forever, the goal is to create something that will.

Chuck Palahniuk

Chapter one

What happens when I die?

There are many variables for what happens when you die, depending upon whether your death was expected or unexpected, where it took place, and the circumstances surrounding your death.

Upon your death it is your executor of your Will who has the most important role to play. If you passed away without a Will it would be your next of kin who would undertake this role. For the purposes of this chapter we will assume that you died leaving a Will so that we may expand on the role that the executor plays in carrying out your final wishes.

THE ROLE OF THE EXECUTOR

Starting from the moment that you die, it is the executor's role to advise the relevant people and organisations of your death. They would need to advise family members, friends, and your employer in the first instance, and this list would expand as the executor progresses through their role. If you leave a list of people who you would like the executor to contact on your death, they will be able to work their way through this list in a timely manner.

The executor would need to liaise with the funeral director to arrange your funeral in accordance with your funeral wishes stipulated in your Will or your personal papers. If no wishes are stipulated, it is at the executor's discretion in respect to what funeral you receive and what happens to your body and how it is disposed of.

Any minor children you have need to be taken care of. If your child's other parent has predeceased you then arrangements would be made for your child to be placed into the care of the guardian you appointed in your Will.

If you had business interests or operated a business then your executor would need to review any instructions and wishes you left behind in respect of the ongoing operations of this business, and ensure that the applicable processes are put in place to facilitate this.

Next, the executor must ensure that all your assets are secured. That all keys are accounted for in respect to property that you may own, together with motor vehicles, boats, caravans, motorbikes and other similar assets. They need to confirm that all these assets are safely stored, and the appropriate insurances are in place for such assets.

Most people would think securing assets would be a simple task for an executor, however let me assure you people do the strangest things at the strangest of times. I vividly recall a frantic phone call from a client early one morning advising that her mother had died at 11pm the night prior. Around two hours later – at 1am – a truck had appeared at her mother's house and her mother's expensive grand piano and elaborate chandeliers were loaded into the truck and driven away. Her sister had determined that with her mother's passing those items should now belong to her and had arranged for the removal, literally within hours of her mother leaving this world. The executor had to act quickly to retrieve those items and restore them to their rightful place under her safe custody.

Your executor must undertake an inventory of all your personal assets and liabilities as at the time of your death. It is important to note that joint assets held by you with another person are treated separately and are not included in your assets for probate purposes. The treatment of joint assets is discussed later in this book (see chapter five). In some cases obtaining an inventory of all of your assets and liabilities can be a relatively simple task if you held minor or simple assets such as one property and a bank account, with minimal personal assets, or if you were prudent and left details of all of your assets and liabilities, which would greatly assist your executor in preparing such an inventory.

In cases where you hold multiple properties, bank accounts, investments, trusts and business structures, if such assets are not clearly documented it may add an element of complication to your executor's role. In which case, your executor must make enquiries with financial institutions, share registries, your accountant and financial advisor to obtain the relevant information.

In respect to properties that you held, your executor would also need to engage the services of a real estate agent to obtain a market appraisal of the value of each property you owned as at the date of your death. This is for both probate purposes and to provide as a record for taxation purposes if required.

Grant of probate

Your executor must obtain a Grant of Probate of your Will if you die leaving personal assets valued at more than $50,000 (in Victoria). Each state within Australia has different processes in respect to their probate requirements and lodgement, so your executor would need to familiarise themselves with the probate requirements of the jurisdiction in which you resided and held assets.

Unless your executor is familiar with such probate processes it would be expedient for them to engage the services of a probate solicitor to assist them with obtaining a Grant of Probate of your Will. On this matter, in my own personal experience, I have had many people come to me after attempting to undertake the process themselves only to realise it is beyond their comprehension and that the time they are investing in something they don't understand is wasted and they finally recognise that an expert who practises in this area day in, day out is the best person to attend to this matter on their behalf.

Asset distribution

Once a successful Grant of Probate of your Will is obtained your executor must administer the estate on behalf of the beneficiaries until such time that the estate is distributed in accordance with the provisions of the deceased's Will. In Victoria, the *Administration and Probate Act* 1958 (Vic.) stipulates that the assets of the estate should not be distributed to the beneficiaries until six months from the date of the Grant of Probate, and if the executor determines to distribute such assets prior to this date then the executor will be personally liable should a claim be brought against the estate and be successful.

If your executor is obtaining a Grant of Probate in another Australian jurisdiction they would need to ascertain the applicable distribution requirements in the jurisdiction in which the probate is obtained so that they do not personally expose themselves to any successful claims brought against the estate.

In administering your estate your executor needs to ensure that the value of the estate does not significantly decrease during the period that they are administering it on behalf of the beneficiaries, and your executor has a strong fiduciary duty to the beneficiaries that they act in their best interests at all times.

It is therefore not prudent for your executor to invest the assets of the estate in highly speculative stocks, hoping for a quick profit. If your executor did in fact do this and the share market crashed depleting the value of your estate, then your executor could very well find themselves being sued by your aggrieved beneficiaries.

In the transition period from when a Grant of Probate is obtained to when your estate is distributed your executor would seek to sell or liquidate the assets of the estate (unless there were specific bequeaths to beneficiaries), and attend to any of your wishes in respect to their business or trust interests.

In some cases, at the expiration of the six-month period from the Grant of Probate, your estate may not be distributed. This may be the case where your Will stipulates that your beneficiaries are to receive their inheritance at a specific age and your beneficiaries are yet to reach that age. In this case your executor would continue to administer that beneficiary's inheritance until they attain the age stipulated in your Will. Your executor could continue the role of executor for a number of years if the beneficiary is particularly young at the time of your death, or if you have included Capital Protective Trusts or Life Interests in your Will.

I hope this overview of the steps that need to occur after your death provide you with some clarification of what happens when you die. Some may not be relevant to your circumstances and some steps may require further clarification when putting your Estate Plan in place, so that you have a more comprehension overview of what needs to take place.

What you leave behind
is not what is engraved in
stone monuments,
but what is woven into
the lives of others.

Pericles

Chapter two

The importance of an Estate Plan

An Estate Plan allows you to stay in the driver's seat.

It allows you to control what happens to all your assets, those that you own and those that you control, when you are no longer here. It allows you to choose who looks after any young children you may have, and most importantly it gives you the opportunity to stipulate how you would like your children to be raised if you are no longer here. If you have business interests or operations, it is an opportunity to stipulate what is to happen to these subsequent to your death – you can provide detailed wishes relating to these interests if you so choose.

Essentially, an Estate Plan allows you to create your legacy, to show your family that you loved them enough to take the time to sit down and put in place your final wishes in respect to your family.

It is also about securing your family's future. In saying this, I am not just referring to your family's financial future. This is important, and if an Estate Plan is put in place correctly then it should ensure your family is looked after financially. If there are some financial deficiencies, and these do arise from time to time, it may be a matter of looking at insurances and perhaps increasing insurance policies or taking out a new insurance policy to ensure that there would be adequate funds if you were to pass away. It could also be rearranging some of the assets you hold that no longer serve you from a financial or estate planning perspective. It could also result in transferring assets to different structures that may be viable and perhaps more tax effective for you.

It is also about keeping the harmony between family members. In short, if you pass away without an Estate Plan you are leaving behind a family that essentially has no written instructions in respect to what was important to you, what you wished for your legacy to be and who you would like to receive all of your worldly or unworldly goods as the case may be.

If you have business interests with no succession plan or agreements in place, then this provides an extra layer of complication. Essentially what you could be leaving behind is a grieving family, highly emotional, facing a new world without you in it, and additional stress as a result of you not putting in place your Will and other estate planning documents that are applicable to your circumstances. In short, it can create devastation, and can quickly diminish once tightly held bonds between family members. For most people that is the last thing they would want to happen, particularly if you have spent considerable time and sacrifice creating and building your wealth and a strong, cohesive family unit.

GETTING STARTED

The process of putting an Estate Plan in place can be more simple than you think. As well as ensuring that your family is adequately looked after, it allows you the opportunity to think about your situation in greater detail and get beneath the surface of many relevant matters. If I had a dollar for every client who said to me after our initial consultation, 'I hadn't thought of that,' I would be a very rich lady indeed.

It firstly allows you to do a thorough inventory of all that you own and owe. Many people drift through life thinking that they don't own that much, but when it's all down on paper in front of them they are actually surprised in respect to what they have accumulated during their life to date.

Choosing your executor

The role of executor is an important role that needs serious consideration. Why? Essentially because you are entrusting them with everything that you own. You are relying on them to follow all your wishes in accordance with the provisions of your Will, and in doing so they have a strong fiduciary duty to act in the best interest of all beneficiaries at all times. If any of the beneficiaries of your Will are young at the time of your death they may not receive their inheritance for a number of years, depending on the age that you stipulated in your Will that they may receive their inheritance. In this case, your executor may be required to look after and control particular beneficiaries' inheritance for several years. As a consequence of this, you need to ensure that you are appointing the best person to undertake this role.

If you have minor children this is often a time of serious reflection, of putting yourself in a situation where you hope you will never be, of passing away while your children are minors and you not being there to guide and care for them. I find this is an emotional stumbling block for many clients, and I totally understand why. It is extremely hard to comprehend a world where you are not there for your children, particularly if your children are young. It is hard to decide who is the best person to care for your children and raise them until they are adults.

Some people's support networks – families and friends – are not nearby; some people have elderly family members who may not be the best people to perform the role of your children's guardian; and some people are estranged from their family. There is also the conundrum that you may wish your children to remain at their current school, as this will provide some stability in their life in terms of structure and friends, however the most appropriate person to be your children's guardian may live an hour away. These are all things that need to be considered when choosing the best person to be your children's guardian.

A Memorandum of Wishes

In addition to making provision in your Will for who will be your executor and who will be your children's guardian, you may also wish to include a Memorandum of Wishes. This letter of wishes provides guidance to the executor in respect to an array of matters. For instance, if you have minor children you may wish to stipulate what type of investments you would like the assets to be invested in; you may also wish to stipulate wishes in respect to your children about their education and schools that they attend. This can be a relatively exhaustive document, depending on your wishes, and is separate from your Will.

You may be in a second marriage where both you and your partner have children from a previous relationship. Depending on how you would like to distribute your assets upon your death this can add a level of complexity that needs to be discussed and worked through. There are several options that can be put in place for blended families to ensure all relevant parties are looked after in accordance with your wishes.

Most parents want to look after their children when they are no longer here, however some people may have adult children who face challenges on their journey through life, whether this be substance abuse or addiction, being a spendthrift, disabled, or the inability to manage money. There are an array of options that can be put in place to accommodate such children, and these should be discussed and explored as part of your Estate Plan.

If you have a business, you may need to make adequate provision in your Will in respect to what happens to your business after your death. You may operate a family business in a company or Trust, and it is integral that adequate provision is made and documented in respect to what happens to this business on your demise. If the business operates through a trading company, who are the shares to pass to? If the business operates in a Family Trust, you need to look at the Trust Deed of the Family Trust to ascertain who the Appointor or Guardian of the Trust is and whether a replacement Appointor or Guardian has been appointed in the Trust Deed. Alternatively, the Trust Deed may allow you to make provision for a replacement Appointor or Guardian in your Will. If your business is a large business with a number of associated parties, do you have a succession plan in place and a succession agreement so that all parties are covered in the event of the incapacity or death of a party?

You may operate your business as a sole trader, however it may be of value and components may be a saleable asset upon your death. I recently acted for a client who operated as a sole trader who had grown her successful business to a significant client base through consistent and dedicated hard work. When putting her Estate Plan in place we left a direction to the executor that they seek the advice of a business professional who was totally across all levels of her business together with a colleague in the industry in which she operated in respect to guidance relating to the sale of components of her business. The reason these people were mentioned is one had in-depth knowledge of her business and the other had in-depth knowledge and contacts within the industry, so if my client were to pass away the executor would be well supported by knowledgeable professionals who could assist him in this regard.

Putting in place an Estate Plan allows you to stipulate your wishes in respect to your final farewell. Some people just like to ensure they have their request to be buried or cremated listed in their Will; some people haven't even thought about what they want to happen to their body upon their passing. To some this is not important, to others it is – it is their last moment to shine and they want to document how the production should run. I have had people come to me with details of where their celebration of life is to take place, the songs, the eulogy, the wake, and everything in between. I have one dear client who insisted that she would like to be cremated with a cup of hot English tea. She drank this every day so thought it would be a fitting way to leave this world.

Power of Attorney details

In addition, putting in place your Power of Attorney documents as part of your Estate Plan allows you to determine who you would like to take care of you and your legal, financial, guardianship and medical matters in the event that you became incapacitated and could no longer make your own decisions.

DIY Wills

One thing that is integral when putting an Estate Plan in place is this: do it properly. Do *not* take shortcuts. It does not matter if your assets are simple or if you have vast assets, business interests, trusts and companies. The same rule applies every time. Take the time to do it correctly and document it properly. During my time as a lawyer, I have seen all sorts of Wills, including an interesting array of DIY Wills. I really do hope to capture the DIY Wills before someone dies, however unfortunately sometimes they don't land on my desk until it's too late and the person has passed.

In obtaining a Grant of Probate, Courts have specific requirements that must be adhered to in respect to the construction of Wills. In Australia, each state is a different probate jurisdiction which can sometimes add a level of confusion and complexity. However, the probate jurisdictions of the applicable Courts do have similar rules in respect to the construction of Wills.

The most common thing that seems to catch many people out with DIY Wills is the absence of revocation and execution clauses and the Will not being witnessed or incorrectly witnessed. Consequently, these DIY Wills can take a little bit of work in the preparation of supplementary documents to satisfy the requirements of the Court. As such, it quite often ends up costing the deceased estate more to fix the deficiencies in the DIY Will than it would have cost if the person had seen an estate planning lawyer while they were alive to put in place a well-documented Will that met their requirements.

Similarly, Will kits that can be purchased from a newsagent or post office can be problematic. If you have business interests, control trusts or have a blended family it's going to be mightily difficult to stipulate your extensive wishes in a pre-formatted Will kit that is not tailored to your specific circumstances.

All the issues discussed in this chapter provide strong foundations on the importance of properly preparing an estate plan and why you should put one in place today.

The best thing an estate plan does is provides clarity and certainty. It may be a challenging journey to get through the process, however I can assure you that you will have peace of mind once it is all finalised and your legacy is in place, and that is something you can't put a price on.

The greatest legacy anyone can leave behind is to positively impact the lives of others. Whenever you add value to other people's lives, you are unknowingly leaving footprints on the sands of time that live on, even after your demise.

Emeasoba George

Chapter three

Appointing your executor

WHO IS YOUR MOST TRUSTED ALLY?

The role of an executor is a crucial one to consider when putting your estate plan in place. In appointing someone as the executor of your Will you are giving them the keys to all that you own and control. That is big. You therefore need to appoint someone you trust implicitly to undertake this role. You need to appoint your most trusted ally.

Appointing your partner or spouse

Most couples appoint each other to be their executor in the first instance. So, if the husband passed away the wife would be the husband's executor and vice versa. This is simple enough. However, if you are single or your spouse or partner does not want to undertake the role of the executor then you need to look further afield to appoint someone as your executor.

Appointing your children

Determining who to choose as an executor can be extremely challenging for many people. Often, they may consider having one or two of their adult children, but at the same time do not want to offend any adult children they may leave out. Often, they may have a sibling that they get along fabulously with, however they are not suitable to undertake the role of an executor or don't have the business acumen and comprehension to do so. Another aspect that I often find clients struggle with is they may want to appoint a particular child as their executor, however they may have another child who is overbearing or manipulative and they have concerns about whether the child they wish to appoint as executor is strong enough to withstand this. These are just some of the many considerations when choosing your executor.

In some instances, particularly where you die leaving behind young children, the role of executor could extend for a considerable number of years. If you pass away leaving a five-year-old child, and you have stipulated in your Will your child is to receive their inheritance when they are twenty-five, your executor would then need to manage your child's entitlement to your estate for the next twenty years.

In other instances, you may put in place a life interest for your partner, allowing them to continue to reside in a residence that you own subsequent to your death, for the rest of their life. Or perhaps you have a child with a dependency issue who cannot control their own money, so you put in place a Capital Protective Trust for your child's benefit, of which the executor is the Trustee. In such cases your executor may need to undertake the role of executor for an extensive period, which could be twenty, thirty years or longer.

Appointing a parent

I have found clients in their thirties and forties who are putting their Will in place quite often wish to appoint their parents as their executor or alternate executor. That is fine; you just need to be conscious that as your parents get older or are no longer the most suitable person to be your executor then you need to make a change in your Will appointing someone else to be your executor or alternate executor.

Appointing joint executors

Often people choose to elect two people as joint executors. If you are giving consideration to having joint executors, it is important to ask yourself what sort of relationship these two people have. Ask yourself, do they get along and where are both executors located? If one is in remote Western Australia and the other in Kakadu, are they necessarily the best people to be an executor of a Will for someone who resided on the eastern seaboard of Australia? Alternatively, they could reside overseas. There is no issue with appointing an executor who is overseas, however you must give consideration to them having to return to Australia to deal with your probate and estate matters, which may require considerable time and cost, flying between Australia and their country of residence.

Recently, I acted for siblings who were the joint executors of their mother's Will. The mother had died in Victoria and a Grant of Probate was obtained in Victoria. Her daughter who was one of the executors of her Will, resided in Queensland while the other executor, a son, resided in Victoria. The daughter had a fear of flying so she was unwilling to fly to Victoria to attend to the execution of documents required for probate and handle other issues, so her brother had to make a number of trips to Queensland with documents so that the probate and estate process could be adhered to.

Fortunately, the brother was willing to fly to Queensland even though he himself had extensive business interests to attend to at home. This is a positive instance of appointing executors who, despite challenges geographically, were willing to work together towards a common goal of obtaining a Grant of Probate and finalising a deceased estate.

There is nothing worse than having two executors who do not get along. I once acted for two brothers who were executors of their father's Will and they had not spoken to each other or been in the same room for twenty years. Let's say it was not pretty. The hostility they held towards each other was still strong, and a simple estate matter was dragged out for considerably longer than it should have been, and probably would still be playing out if it were not for my interference.

On another occasion I acted for two sisters, let us call them Jill and Prue, who were appointed by their father as the joint executors of his Will. The relationship between the sisters had been frosty for a period but they had managed to make amends just prior to their father passing away. Unfortunately, the role of executor was a testing one for them as each of the sisters liked to assume control, and invariably the relationship broke down. It was left to me to be the conduit between the warring sisters in respect to the estate matters, to the point where I had to orchestra the collection and exchange of certain sentimental items between the parties.

One of those items was their father's ashes. Prue had demanded her father's ashes be handed over to her and rather remarkably Jill willingly obliged. It was arranged that the father's ashes would be delivered to our office at 3 o'clock one Friday afternoon by Jill and then Prue would collect them at 3.30pm on the same day. A smooth process indeed. The ashes were dropped off as arranged by Jill – however at 3.30 Prue was nowhere to be seen.

The clock was ticking rapidly towards 5pm and, despite some frantic telephone calls and emails, we could not get hold of Prue. Our office was closed over the weekend, and although we hold a variety of items on safe custody for our clients, ashes of dead people is not one of them. We found a hiding spot for the ashes, as I had terrible visions of the office being broken into and the ashes being stolen or the office burning down, something which has never happened prior to or after this day.

Suffice to say it was an uneasy weekend, and we were mighty glad to hand the ashes over to Prue when she finally surfaced at our office the following Monday morning.

The moral of this story is that if your children don't get along it's probably not ideal for them to be your joint executors, as it could be detrimental to both them and other parties, and maybe even the lawyer representing them in your probate matter.

If you are considering appointing joint executors, I encourage you to give these issues some serious thought:

- Do they know each other?
- Will they work well together as joint executors of your Will?

- Is there any conflict between them?
- Will they focus on your wishes and the best interests of the beneficiaries of your Will?

Likewise, having executors who reside overseas can also add a level of complexity, particularly when dealing with probate matters and the sale and liquidation of estate assets. If there are ideal candidates within Australia who you feel comfortable appointing as your executor, that would usually be preferred to appointing someone who resides overseas.

If you have business interests or operate your own business, you may wish to consider someone who has business acumen and an understanding of your business operations to undertake the role. If the person you would like to appoint as your executor does not have business acumen, however you strongly feel that they are the best person for the role, that is perfectly fine. In this case I would strongly recommend that you give consideration to leaving directions in your Will or a Memorandum of Wishes in respect to who your executor should consult or seek advice from in respect to your business interests.

Essentially, when appointing an executor of your Will the person you appoint is the person that you trust the most who you feel has the attributes and capacity to undertake this role in the best interests of you and your beneficiaries.

Please think about your legacy because you're writing it everyday.

Gary Vaynerchuck

Chapter four

The importance of trusted advisors

During our lifetime many of us rely on the counsel of trusted advisors, whether they be accountants, financial advisors, lawyers, stockbrokers, business advisors or insurance agents. For some of us, we may develop a strong relationship with one or more trusted advisors over many years and therefore our advisors may possess intimate knowledge in respect to a specific area of your business and personal matters.

If you are a business owner that operates one or more businesses you may have built strong trusted relationships with an accountant, who aside from attending to your quarterly and yearly accounts, may also be across your tax planning, business projections and forecasting, as well as distributions to family trusts together with in-depth knowledge of your business entities and any other trusts or investments that you may control or own during your lifetime.

Likewise, your financial advisor is likely to have a strong understanding of all your investments and how all your assets are structured, together with current values of investment portfolios.

Depending on the complexity of your estate, the assets that you hold and the structures that you have established to hold these assets, it may take some time for your executor to gain a full comprehension of your business structures, personal assets, joint assets, together with assets that you controlled in trusts at the time of your death.

Given this, it is highly recommended that when putting your Will in place you list your current advisors and stipulate that you would like your executor to seek the advice of your advisors upon your death. This will enable your executor to meet with your advisors after your death and gain a comprehensive overview of your assets and structures.

BEING ABLE TO WORK TOGETHER

Your executor may have meetings with your advisors and determine that they do not gel, and may determine to seek the advice of their own advisors going forward. That is fine, however by specifying in your Will your current advisors your executor has an invaluable resource to seek guidance in respect of your estate, your personal trust, business and any other assets.

In some instances, you may operate a business in which you are the key person, and with you no longer here the best outcome may be that the business is sold. Frequently when I am putting estate plans in place for my clients who operate a business that they determine would need to be sold on their demise, they request that we stipulate the names of people they would like their executor to seek the advice from in respect to the sale of their business in their Will or Memorandum of Wishes.

Your executor may be someone with business acumen, however they may not be familiar with the industry in which you operated your business or the key players and issues pertaining to that industry. By providing them with guidance on who to seek advice from in respect to the sale of your business, they will have the opportunity to gain the appropriate advice and be in a better position to sell your business and obtain an appropriate financial outcome in respect to the sale.

Trusted advisors can be extremely valuable, not only during your lifetime but also subsequent to your death, when they are able to play an important role in advising your executor and loved ones in respect to your business, trust and personal assets, thus providing an invaluable resource at an emotional and challenging time.

Enjoy the little things, for one day you may look back and realise they were the big things.

Robert Brault

Chapter five

Joint assets

JOINT OWNERSHIP

Owning assets jointly is extremely common. Many couples own joint assets for ease of management. The most common assets that people jointly own are property and bank accounts.

In respect to bank accounts which are jointly held, these accounts will pass to the surviving account holder at the time of the death of a joint account holder. The surviving account holder will need to take a certified copy of the deceased's death certificate to the bank as confirmation that the deceased has passed. The deceased's name will be removed from the bank account and the surviving partner will continue to have full access and use of that bank account.

It is commonplace for spouses to have joint accounts during their lifetime, which easily transfer to the survivor upon the death of either of them.

In recent years I have seen the emergence of joint accounts being held by a parent and an adult child. For one reason or another a joint bank account is established in both the parent and adult child's name using the parent's funds. Often, the parent may be elderly and may not have good mobility, and is reliant on their adult child to assist them with the payment of bills and other financial matters.

Many elderly parents do not comprehend that upon their death the funds in this account will pass to the adult child who is the joint account holder. Rather they think the funds in the bank account will be dealt with in accordance with the provisions of their Will, which is not the case. Often, it is not until the death of the elderly parent that other family members are aware of this account, and there is often little recourse given that the bank account is a joint asset.

In respect to property, if property is held between you and your spouse as joint proprietors then at the time of the death of your spouse you, as the joint proprietor, will receive your spouse's share in the property and will be the sole proprietor of the property. This property would not form part of your spouse's estate. Even if your spouse had made provision for this property in their Will, such provisions would not be enforceable as the property was held as a joint asset, not an individual asset.

However, if you hold a property as tenants in common with one or more people then your share of the property will be dealt with in accordance with the provisions of your Will. The people who you owned such property with will not be entitled to your share unless you have provided for this in your Will.

TENANTS IN COMMON

The important thing to consider when owning assets as tenants in common is, what is your intention for the asset when you are no longer here?

Owning a property as tenants in common with a partner is common in second marriages, where one or both partners have children from previous relationships. You may acquire a residence where it is intended that you will both reside in the property until such time that you are both no longer here, at which time the residence would be sold and your share in the property will be distributed in accordance with the provisions of your Will, while your partner's share in the property will be distributed in accordance with the provisions of their Will.

To allow the surviving spouse to remain in the property upon the death of the first spouse, provision would have to be made in their respective Wills, providing each other with a life interest or right to occupy the property. This means that they can reside in the property for the remainder of their life, and then upon the death of the survivor the property is sold.

Owning a property as tenants in common is something that needs to be carefully considered. If you and your partner own a property as tenants in common and do not intend to make provision in your respective Wills to leave each other a life interest or right to occupy then at the time of your death the property may need to be sold to ensure that your equity in the property can be distributed to your beneficiaries in accordance with your Will.

Alternatively, you may make provision in your Will that your partner has the first option to acquire the property should they so wish to do so. In doing so you would need to provide very clear parameters in respect to the time frame that must be adhered to, together with the process for determining the market valuation of the property.

There are a number of valuation methodologies, including a sworn valuation, an agreed valuation between both of you at the time of putting your Will in place, or directing your executor to obtain three property appraisals from real estate agents familiar with the area where the property is located which are then averaged to provide a market value.

The above-mentioned process in respect to providing someone with a first right of refusal to acquire your equity in a property can apply to anyone with whom you own property as tenants in common; it is not restricted to a partner. So, if you owned property with a child, a friend or business associate the same principle could apply.

Joint assets are assets that should still be considered in your estate plan. They are important to consider when putting your estate plan in place, particularly as it will help you to identify what assets will pass to each beneficiary and which assets will pass to people by way of owning joint assets with you.

Someone is sitting in the shade today because someone planted a tree a long time ago.

Warren Buffett

Chapter six

Personal vs trust assets

An important aspect of putting in place your Estate Plan is to know where all your assets live. You may have some assets that you own personally, some in a company, you may control some assets as a consequence of being the appointor or guardian of a trust, you may also be a unit holder of assets held by a Unit Trust, and you may have superannuation and life insurance.

All the different types of assets that I mentioned in the previous paragraph need to be dealt with in isolation when looking at putting in place your Estate Plan.

PERSONAL ASSETS

In respect to your personal assets, which are assets that are owned in your own individual name, provision for these assets can be made in your Will. These typically include your residence, investment property, holiday home, cars, furniture and personal chattels, shares, boats, caravans and so forth. Some say these can be the easiest assets to deal with as you can determine who you would like to receive each asset and make provisions for such assets in your Will.

It is important to note that when we are talking about assets that you personally own in your own name, we are not referring to any joint assets that you may own with another party (see chapter five). These are purely assets that you personally own by yourself.

It is common for people to hold shares in a trading company. Such companies could own assets, or perhaps it is the vehicle that you operate your business in. As these shares are a personal asset you may make provision in your Will in respect to these shares and who these shares are to pass to at the time of your death. This means that if you own a property in a company, by leaving someone the shares in that company you are effectively leaving them the property.

TRUST ASSETS

Trust assets are treated differently to personal assets, as effectively you do not personally own these assets, the Trust owns the assets. As such, you cannot make specific provision for these assets in your Will in the same manner that you would for assets that you personally own.

Let us say Jack had a Discretionary Trust, which is a trust that many people commonly refer to as a Family Trust. In this trust Jack owns two properties, some shares and some cash held in a bank account. Jack cannot stipulate in his Will who he would like to leave each asset in the trust to as he does not personally own these assets. Jack may be the Guardian or Appointor of the Discretionary Trust, which effectively means he is the person who has effective control of these assets and can decide who receives any benefit from the trust, whether this be distributions from the trust or assets.

If you have a Discretionary Trust, it is imperative that you look at the schedule of the Trust Deed to ascertain who the Appointor or Guardian is. As previously mentioned, the person appointed as the Appointor or Guardian of a Discretionary Trust has total control over the trust, and it is at their total discretion as to who receives any benefits from such a trust.

The schedule contained in the Trust Deed may make provision for a replacement Appointor or Guardian to be named at the time of the original Appointor's or Guardian's death, or the Trust Deed may make provision for the current Appointor or Guardian to make provision in their Will appointing a new Appointor or Guardian of the trust upon their death.

If such a provision is contained in the Trust Deed allowing you to appoint a new Appointor or Guardian of the trust upon your death then you may make provision in your Will to appoint someone as your replacement Appointor or Guardian of your Discretionary Trust, effectively giving them control of your trust assets when you are no longer here. Once that person has assumed the role of Appointor or Guardian subsequent to your death, it is entirely up to them in respect to what happens to the assets of the Discretionary Trust and who receives any distributions from the trust.

If there were certain assets held by the Discretionary Trust that you wished to go to certain individuals, you may put in place a Memorandum of Wishes in place stipulating what your wishes are in respect to the assets held by the Discretionary Trust. This Memorandum of Wishes is not legally binding on the new Appointor or Guardian, however we do find that in most cases it is often highly persuasive and has a positive effect on your wishes being adhered to.

It is common for businesses to be operated in a Discretionary Trust. If you have a family business which is to pass to a family member at the time of your death then provision should be made for the control of this trust to pass to them at the time of your death. In saying this, I am referring to this distribution in isolation and not looking holistically at the whole distribution of your estate and the impact of this provision on other family members. The distribution of whole estates, particularly in respect to family businesses, is discussed in chapter ten, Family Businesses and Maintaining the Harmony.

If, however, you hold other assets such as property in your trust in addition to operating your business in the trust, you would need to give extensive consideration to these assets when putting your estate plan in place.

Unit Trusts are another type of trust that are utilised in Australia. They are fixed trusts, where the Trustee holds the assets of the trust for the benefit of the unit holders. Unit Trusts are often used where unrelated parties purchase property or operate a business together. When putting an estate plan in place you need to give consideration in respect to what happens to your units in the Unit Trust at the time of your death. If you own the units personally then you may make provision for who receives these units in your Will.

If, however, a company owns these units you would then need to make provision for who is to receive the shares in the company that holds the units. Alternatively, perhaps these units are an asset of your Discretionary Trust, in which case you will need to consider them when reviewing all the assets of your Discretionary Trust.

Superannuation is another asset that catches people out, frequently. Many think that you can make provision for superannuation in your Will. Superannuation is an asset that you do not personally own at the time of your death, it is an asset that is held on trust for you by the trustee of your Superannuation Fund, whether that Fund be a Master Fund, Industry Fund, Self-Managed Superannuation Fund or otherwise. Anyone who has superannuation needs to provide a direction to the trustee of their superannuation fund in respect to what they would like to happen to their superannuation at the time of their death. Such direction or nomination is usually referred to as a Binding Death Nomination and further information on such nominations and the payment of superannuation are provided in chapter twelve, of this book, Get Your Super Right.

Frequently, superannuation is directed to be paid to a spouse, partner or children, in which case it does not have any impact on your estate. However, if you have stipulated in your Binding Death Nomination that you would like your superannuation paid to your estate or your legal personal representative then your superannuation would form part of your estate and then be paid in accordance with the provisions of your Will. If you do not have a Binding Death

Nomination in place the trustee of your Superannuation Fund may pay your superannuation to your estate, dependent upon the provisions of the Superannuation Trust Deed and whether or not you had any dependants at the time of your death.

It is therefore imperative that you do make some form of provision in your Will for how you would like your superannuation distributed.

We are fortunate that today we have the luxury of holding assets in a variety of different vehicles that best suit our circumstances. The offset to this is that we need to consider all these different vehicles when deciding our legacy and who we would like to leave our legacy to. With the right advice and guidance, you can adequately capture both your personal assets and trust assets, allowing you to put in place a well-documented Estate Plan.

Legacy is not what's left tomorrow when you're gone. It's what you give, create, impact and contribute today while you're here that then happens to live on.

Rasheed Ogunlaru

Chapter seven

Do an inventory of assets and liabilities

Let us imagine for a moment that your closest friend died suddenly and unexpectedly. Your friend and his wife gone forever, leaving behind two teenage children, successful business interests, a substantial investment portfolio and various other assets – and no comprehensive records of everything.

You are the executor of his Will. Where do you start? What do you do first? How do you know what assets your friend owned and what liabilities he left behind?

Stop and imagine yourself in this position. How would it make you feel? Overwhelmed by the task ahead, anxious, frustrated? Perhaps all of those.

The whole point of this exercise was to put in perspective what happens if you don't leave your affairs in an orderly manner, to realise how helpless and frustrated you would feel if somebody did this to you, and to hopefully motivate and encourage you to ensure that your own executor is not left to feel this way upon your death.

I'm a big advocate for documenting *everything*; the easier you can make it for those left behind the better. Trust me, those left behind will thank you for it.

KEEP IT SIMPLE

When putting everything in place you do not need to put in place an array of fancy convoluted lists: a nice simple spreadsheet will suffice. When entering your assets into the spreadsheet it would be ideal to separate them in accordance with how each individual asset is owned. By this I mean, list all your personal assets together, remembering that personal assets are assets that you personally own in your own name. You may also own some assets jointly with a spouse or friend; list those assets as another separate category. If you own property jointly with someone who is not your spouse, it would be ideal to list the name of the person who you own these assets with and whether the asset is owned as joint proprietors or tenants in common.

If you control trust assets, for example assets held in a Discretionary Trust or Unit Trust, these assets should also be listed. Likewise, if you operate a business in one or more companies that hold assets, these assets should be separately listed under the relevant company name.

Most people have superannuation which is held in trust for them by the trustee of their superannuation fund, so the name of the superannuation fund should also be provided on this list.

Once the list of assets has been tackled, it is time to move on to any liabilities that you may have. This can include mortgages, car loans, personal loans, business loans, credit cards and so on. Again, it would be ideal to break these down to personal liabilities and joint liabilities.

At the end of this chapter a template of an Inventory of Assets and Liabilities is provided to assist you in putting in place your own Inventory of Assets and Liabilities, which would allow your executor to gain a firm overview of the assets that you own, those that you control and any liabilities that you may owe at the time of your death.

Having such an inventory of assets and liabilities in place effectively gives your executor a snapshot of your estate and where each asset lives. It will also save them an inordinate amount of time and energy in gathering all the relevant information they require and collating it for probate and estate purposes.

There have been occasions where I have acted for clients who have not been able to ascertain which bank their mother or father who had died held accounts with. This resulted in us making enquiries with multiple banking institutions to ascertain whether in fact their deceased parent held a current account with them. It is a process which takes time, and is a process that can be alleviated by having everything appropriately listed.

I once acted for a client whose mother had died leaving a rather substantial estate. Some eighteen months after the grant of his mother's probate he received correspondence in respect to some shares that his mother had held. He had no idea that she owned such a substantial holding of shares until that correspondence was received, and he may never have known on the off chance the correspondence was not received. It highlights the importance of your assets being listed and documented.

MAKING CHANGES

It is important that once this list of your assets and liabilities is in place, should there be any changes to any of your asset holdings, that you update the list so that it is current.

In respect to where to keep this list, it would be prudent to keep a copy with your Will. In my practice, clients frequently provide us with copies of their Inventory of Assets and Liabilities to place with their Wills that we hold on safe custody for them in our Deeds Register. These are filed away, and only handed over to the executor after the death of a client.

It would also be ideal to leave a copy of this list among your personal papers as well for easy initial reference for your executor.

Some of my clients are quite comprehensive in the details they leave on this list, listing bank account numbers, shareholding HIN numbers, amount of funds in bank accounts (for consistent accounts such as term deposits) and approximate valuation of assets. You do not necessarily have to go to this level, however if you do, make sure that such a completed list is kept in a secure place given the sensitivity and security of some of the information contained on such list.

Your executors are being gracious in undertaking the role of your executor, particularly if your estate consists of a variety of different classes of assets and trusts. I am sure they would be most appreciative of being left an overview of what your assets and liabilities are and where they all fit into the puzzle. Leaving them an Inventory of Assets and Liabilities will provide them with a comprehensive roadmap to assist them greatly in undertaking their role as your executor.

Inventory of Assets and Liabilities
Hamish and Sophia

PERSONAL ASSETS

Hamish Personal Assets	ANZ Bank Account held at Armadale Branch Term Deposit
	2015 Range Rover Registration Number 1GF5HG
	Harley Davidson Motorbike
Sophia Personal Assets	2017 Q4 Audi Registration Number AAK524
	Investment Property – 44 Smith Street, Fitzroy

JOINT ASSETS

Hamish and Sophia's Joint Assets	Commonwealth Bank Account held at Toorak Branch Goal Saver Account
	ANZ Bank Account held at Armadale Branch Savings Account
	Residence at 4 High Street, Middle Park
	Household Chattels and personal effects
Hamish and his brother Tom's Joint Asset	5 Ocean Road Sorrento (Tenants in Common in Equal Shares)

BUSINESS

Business Operations	Shares in Bayside Builders Pty Ltd are owned by the Hamish and Sophia Family Trust Assets comprise: Commonwealth Bank Business Account held at Toorak Branch Premises at 22 Burwood Road, Hawthorn

LIFE INSURANCE

Hamish	Colonial Insurance Policy No 276765
Sophia	Colonial Insurance Policy No 276665

SUPERANNUATION

Hamish	CBUS No. 1155224
Sophia	Australian Super No. 689254

LIABILITIES

Sophia Personal Liability	Mortgage with Macquarie Bank in relation to Investment Property – 44 Smith Street, Fitzroy
Sophia and Hamish's Joint Liability	Mortgage with ANZ Bank in relation to Residence at 4 High Street, Middle Park
	ANZ Credit Card

It’s the journey that matters, soak it in. Learn lessons out of it. Impact positively so that if you never get to your destination at least you’d leave a legacy to be remembered.

Emem Uko

Chapter eight

International assets

These days it is extremely common to own assets that are not held in Australia – that is, the assets are held overseas – and hence are international assets. Over the last decade, it has become increasingly common for clients to enquire if they can make provision in their Australian Will for assets owned in international jurisdictions.

The short answer is that it depends on where the assets are held.

INTERNATIONAL WILLS

Australia is a party to the UNIDROIT Convention Providing a Uniform Law on the form of an International Will. This essentially means that Australia and other countries who are signatories to the convention mutually accept the validity of international Wills. An international Will allows you to make provision for your overseas assets in your Australian Will.

There are several processes that must be adhered to when putting in place an international Will. Most importantly, it needs to be executed in a manner that complies with both the convention and the jurisdiction in which the Will is made. By way of example, if the Will is executed in Victoria, it must satisfy the provisions of the convention as well as the provisions of Victorian law.

The Will must be executed in the presence of three people: two independent witnesses over the age of eighteen and an authorised witness. An authorised witness is a solicitor or notary public. In addition to witnessing the Will, the authorised witnesses must also complete a certificate in accordance with the provisions and obligations of the convention. It is therefore prudent if you are intending to put an international Will in place that you should have it prepared by an estate planning lawyer familiar with international Wills.

The countries that are a signatory to the UNIDROIT Convention are:

- Australia
- Belgium
- Bosnia-Herzegovina
- Canada
- Croatia
- Cyprus
- Ecuador
- France
- Holy See
- Iran
- Italy
- Laos
- Libya
- Niger
- Portugal
- Russian Federation
- Sierra Leone
- Slovenia
- United Kingdom
- United States of America.

Although your overseas assets may be held in countries that allow you to put an international Will in place, careful consideration of the process must be undertaken prior to doing so.

In my legal practice, I recently put an international Will in place for a client who had substantial personal assets in Victoria and a sole bank account in the United Kingdom. I discussed the process with my client, including the value of the funds in the bank account and where she would like these funds to be paid. Based on these discussions, it seemed logical to put an international Will in place given her circumstances.

MORE COMPLICATED ESTATES

However, there are circumstances where it is perhaps not ideal to put in place an international Will. I once acted for a client who had substantial Australian assets which we made provision for in his Will. In addition to his Australian assets he also had substantial personal, business and trust assets in the United States and Italy. We met the provisions required to put an international Will in place for him. However, his international assets were not of a nominal value: they were hugely significant.

In this case we had to consider the local procedures for probate and asset administration in the United States and Italy. We also had to consider the tax implications, inclusive of any applicable inheritance tax in those countries. It was concluded that it was paramount that my client received the relevant expertise of estate planning lawyers as well as tax experts in both the United States and Italy, so that the correct informed decisions could be made pertaining to our client's international assets held in those jurisdictions. Yes, it may sound cumbersome to have separate Wills in place pertaining to the assets our client held in each jurisdiction, but this is all done to protect our client's best interests. Australia, United States and Italy all have very different legal systems. At the end of the day our client's wishes could be best achieved by having these separate Wills in place in the countries where these assets were held.

If you hold small assets overseas, an international Will may be an appropriate vehicle for you. However, if you hold significant or complex overseas assets it may be in your best interest to put in place a Will in the country where those assets are held.

As detailed earlier in this chapter, an international Will has more extensive requirements than just putting in place a normal Australian Will. If these requirements are not adhered to then the Will that you put in place may not meet the provisions and obligations of the convention and it would then likely be deemed that no valid international Will is in place. If you are seeking to put an international Will in place it is highly recommended that you engage the services of an estate planning lawyer.

If you hold assets in a country that is not a party to the convention you will need to put in place a Will in the country where the assets are held. It is common for many older family members who have migrated to Australia from their country of birth to have retained assets in their original homeland, whether that be bank accounts or property, particularly property owned with other family members. Often it is not until they have passed that their children are fully aware of these assets, and are sent down a rabbit warren trying to claim them in a foreign jurisdiction which can be a time-consuming and costly process.

So a little tip, if you have parents who have migrated to Australia, ask them now if they still have assets in their motherland, and if they do, actively encourage them to put a Will in place in respect to those assets that adheres to the jurisdiction in which they are held. Additionally, if you own assets in jurisdictions that are not a party to the convention, ensure you too put a Will in place to cater for the assets in that jurisdiction.

With the world becoming more accessible and people having assets and business interests globally, it is important to consider all the jurisdictions where your assets are held when putting in place your Estate Plan, and to ensure that they are sufficiently catered for in either an international Will or specific Wills pertaining to each jurisdiction where your assets are held.

Life is full of opportunity. Leadership is about taking those opportunities. Legacy is what you will leave behind when you do.

Jamie Munson

Chapter nine

Taking care of business

For some people, their business is a significant asset in their asset pool, and as such needs to be carefully considered when putting an estate plan in place. There are a number of ways in which to operate your business, and the structure in which your business operates will determine how provision is made for this asset in your estate plan.

Whether your business structure is a personal asset or whether it is something that you control through a trust structure will determine whether provision is made for this asset in your Will or some other estate plan document.

Below are the most common forms of business ownership and the manner in which you may allow for them in your estate plan.

SOLE PROPRIETOR

If you operate your business as a sole proprietor, your business will be an individual asset and would form part of your estate at the time of your death. As such, any business assets are likely to be included in your pool of assets and distributed in accordance with the provisions of your Will. You may, however, make provision in your Will for the business assets to pass to a particular beneficiary should you wish.

One of my clients operates a thriving landscaping business as a sole proprietor. The business operates under a business name, and the client has purchased a car, trailer, gardening equipment and tools to enable him to operate his business. He instructed that he felt his partner could continue to operate his landscaping business subsequent to his death, and made provision in his Will stipulating that at the time of his death his car, trailer, gardening equipment and tools were to pass to his partner so that she may carry on his business.

Another client is a speech pathologist. At the time of her death, given that she works independently with no staff, her business will cease to operate. This client does however have an extensive client list and database that she has accumulated over many years working in her profession, which she believes is of value and is a saleable asset. She has therefore made provision in her Will that her executor is to liaise with two particular industry colleagues to seek their guidance of prospective likeminded industry professionals who may be interested in acquiring her client list and database.

COMPANY

It is common for many businesses to operate as a straight trading company, in which you may be both the director and shareholder. Depending on the size of your business operations, there may also be other directors and shareholders of the company.

Let's say that you operate the business in a company and are the sole director and shareholder. In such case, you would make provision in your Will for who you would like to receive the shares in your business. By transferring the shares, you will also be transferring the assets that are held by the business. Such assets may include stock, motor vehicles, equipment and property, among other things.

One of your children may work in the business with you and it may be your intention that at the time of your death this child is to receive your business. In this case, you would make provision in your Will for your shares in the business to pass to the child who works in the business at the time of your death.

Another client operates a successful plumbing company. There are two directors and shareholders, being my client and his business partner, and a staff of thirty-five. This is where it becomes a little tricky. Many people would assume that the shares in this company would pass to my client's wife upon his death. However, I don't think my client's business partner would be too keen to run a business with my client's wife, who has no business acumen, particularly in respect to operating a plumbing company, nor is she willing to get her hands dirty learning the ropes as an apprentice plumber.

My client and his business partner had some years ago put in place a buy–sell agreement in respect to their business. The business had taken out adequate insurance for both, which means upon the death of my client insurance proceeds would be paid to my client's estate in accordance with the provisions of the buy–sell agreements. The amount of such insurance proceeds would have been agreed by my client and his business partner and adequately documented in the buy–sell agreement.

In exchange for these insurance proceeds my client's shares would be transferred to his business partner. My client's business partner would thereon retain full control of the business in which my client had once held shares, and his estate would have been adequately compensated for the transfer of the shares by way of the insurance proceeds.

It is important when making provisions in your Estate Plan for shares that you hold in companies that you adequately address any shareholders' agreements, partnership agreements, buy–sell agreements, or any other agreements that you may have in place with the relevant parties.

If you operate a business as a partnership or with another unrelated party and do not currently have any succession plans in place, it would be prudent for you to sit down and have discussions with the other parties and talk openly and frankly about what each parties' expectations are in respect to your business in the event of one party becoming incapacitated or dying. Once you have had these open and transparent conversations with each other you really should give consideration to putting your succession plans in place, whether this be by a shareholders' agreement, buy–sell agreement or another form of agreement between the parties.

Simply making provisions for your shares in your Will without giving consideration to any relevant agreements that you may have in place may lead to a conflict situation, and problems that would need to be addressed by your executor and other relevant parties when you are no longer here.

DISCRETIONARY TRUSTS

Often business owners operate their business in a Discretionary Trust. A company may be the trustee of the Discretionary Trust in which they are the director and shareholder of this company. The Discretionary Trust holds the assets.

The most important role in respect to Discretionary Trusts is that of the Appointor or Guardian of the Discretionary Trust. The Appointor or Guardian is the person who determines who receives any distribution from the Trust and who receives the assets of the Trust.

The schedule contained in the Trust Deed of a Discretionary Trust may make provision for a replacement Appointor or Guardian to be appointed at the time of the original Appointor's or Guardian's death. Alternatively, the Trust Deed may make provision for the current Appointor or Guardian to make provision in their Will appointing a new Appointor or Guardian of the Trust upon their death.

If such provision is contained in the Trust Deed allowing you to appoint a new Appointor or Guardian of the trust upon your death, then you may make provision in your Will to appoint someone as your replacement Appointor or Guardian of your Discretionary Trust, effectively giving them control of your Trust assets when you are no longer here.

So if you operated a business with your son and you wished for him to receive the business subsequent to your death then you would make provision for him to be appointed the replacement Appointor or Guardian of the Discretionary Trust. This is a relatively straightforward process if the only assets of the Discretionary Trust are the business assets.

If there are additional assets of the Discretionary Trusts not related to the business, inclusive of property or shareholdings, then these need to be carefully considered when putting in place your estate plan. They may need to be transferred out of the Discretionary Trust into another structure so that they are isolated from the business assets, however careful consideration needs to be given to any capital gains implications and stamp duty implications.

It is therefore prudent to obtain the appropriate financial, legal and accounting advice when instigating the succession planning of your business assets and your estate plan so that the appropriate strategies can be implemented that are in the best interests of you and your proposed beneficiaries.

We have touched on the most common ways that business owners and entrepreneurs operate their business in this chapter with the aim to highlight to you that there are a number of aspects to give consideration to when determining what will happen to your business interests when you are no longer here.

Success isn't just what you accomplish in your life, it's about what you inspire others to do.

Author Unknown

Chapter ten

Family businesses and maintaining family harmony

The most important thing in respect to family businesses and succession plans is being completely transparent with all family members in respect to what the future holds and how the family business will operate. Each family member is likely to have different expectations in respect to what will happen to the family business in the future, so it's important not to let this become the elephant in the room.

DIFFERENT FAMILY EXPECTATIONS

Important discussions need to be had individually and collectively with family members and everyone's expectations must be laid bare. Everyone deserves transparency about what the future holds for them and for their role in the family business.

Some time ago we acted for a family farming business. The father was the patriarch, the mother – due to declining health and the onset of dementia – no longer had a role in the business. The daughter had over a period of time assisted in an administrative capacity in the business, however she had subsequently relocated to the city and was employed independently of the family business, although her father paid the rent on her accommodation. The two sons assisted their father with the farming operations, with one taking on a more dominant role in both farming and business activities. The sons tolerated each other but there was no great love between them.

We had discussions with all members of the family individually, and not surprisingly some home truths came out. The dominant son had no desire to work with his brother once his father was no longer around, as he felt his brother was lazy and he himself was burdened with most of the business operations, which he did not mind so long as he alone was adequately rewarded for his hard work. His brother, not surprisingly, was happy to keep things going as they were. The daughter was not interested in partaking in the family business at any time in the future, however would have been happy to receive a small parcel of farmland and sufficient funds to purchase a city residence.

After speaking with our client's children, we engaged in very open and frank discussions with our client, as he had not been aware of his children's sentiments. It was not something he had previously discussed with them either individually or jointly.

It became apparent to our client that the business and farming operations could not continue in the current manner on his demise without the increasing prospect of conflict between family members. So further discussions were had with all family members in respect to what land parcels they would each like to receive and other expectations they had in respect to the business operations and to their inheritance.

After some manoeuvring between the client's children and our client regarding which land parcels they each wished to ultimately acquire, and how the business operations were to be carried out going forward, a succession plan was laid out. It was not all plain sailing though as some of the land was held in several different trusts, some of which had to be transferred out to other entities, and then there was the issue of ensuring the Appointorship of each trust was adequately covered. In addition, we had to be mindful of any taxation implications as a result of such transfers.

To achieve this successful result we had to look at the client's individual assets, company assets, Discretionary Trust assets, Unit Trust assets and superannuation to ascertain where each asset was held and how we could leave the assets and control of the assets to the next generation in the manner that our client desired and that would not cause disharmony in the family.

In addition, our client's accountant and financial advisor were actively involved in several meetings to provide the necessary financial and taxation advice to our client. It was a mammoth task, but the end result was that we were able to put our client's final wishes in place, in a manner so that his children had total transparency regarding what would happen upon their parent's death and they were satisfied with the way the family business and other assets were to be distributed.

The story I have just described to you is a happy client story, which occurred because the family – and in particular the parents – understood the importance of putting a succession plan in place and listening to the relevant expert advice.

Do not be fooled. Not all stories end in this manner.

DISCORD IN THE FAMILY

On another occasion I assisted in acting for a gentleman who ran a family property developer business. He too had three children: a daughter and two sons. His sons despised each other and were reluctant to attend family meetings at our office as they did not want to be in the same room. Given the father was elderly, the sister was the conduit between her brothers.

My client was immensely proud of what he had achieved and rightly so, as he had built up an extremely successful business. My client did not under any circumstances wish for any part of his business operations to be separated, despite the fact there was more than enough to go around and a segregation of assets and operations could have occurred – no such segregation occurred.

I'm not sure if my client honestly thought that his two sons who had despised each other for so many years would miraculously start to get along upon his demise, but he was ruling with an iron fist in respect to the business succession plans, much to the detriment of his family.

Having been around long enough, I know that if siblings do not get along when a parent is alive then they have Buckley's chance of getting along when that parent is no longer here. It is normally the parent who is the glue that holds the family together; without that glue that bond can be diminished.

I often hear clients comment that they do not care what happens when they are no longer here. It's a comment that I admit irritates me at the best of times, as I know the potential conflict and anguish that can arise as a result of them not putting any succession plans in place, or putting inadequate succession plans in place.

I think the reason people say they do not care what happens when they are no longer here is that it's too hard for them to think about what to put in place. They do not know where to start, they don't fully understand the family dynamics or what other family members' expectations are in respect to the business. It is hard making tough decisions and having difficult conversations, but once it is all laid out on the table and put in place, everyone is on the same page and can confidently move forward knowing where the future of the family business lies.

Another aspect of family business that I often see is where one child has worked in the family business and other children have not. What happens to this business on your death can be a contentious issue. The child who works in the business may have an expectation that the business will be left to them. However, your expectation may be different. It is ideal to be transparent with all children, whatever the case. It may be your intention that the child who works in the business does receive the business upon your death and your remaining children may receive equivalent assets from your estate or superannuation.

It is important that if you are leaving a business to one of your children and equivalent assets to other children with the intention that they each receive an equal share of your estate that you clearly stipulate a valuation clause in respect to the business in your Will. This will go a long way to alleviating any conflict that the business is valued too low or high as your executor will need to abide by the valuation methodology provided in your Will. Your remaining children would then receive assets of equivalent value, and then any estate assets more than this value would be divided equally between all your children.

When conversing with business owners at our preliminary estate planning meeting, they sometimes raise the prospect that they would like all children to share in the business even though all of their children may not work in the business. The son may work in the business, doing long hours, and his three sisters may not be involved in the business in any shape or form. The client will often say that they want the business to be split equally between their four children, regardless of whether the business is operated as a company or in a trust.

We need to kindly draw the client's attention to conceptualise what their son who works tediously long hours in the business would think of our client's intentions regarding the business. He does all the hard work, yet he only reaps a quarter of the profits, while his three siblings who do not partake in the business receive seventy-five percent of the profits between them. I would not mind being one of those sisters. The reality in most cases is that this structure is not feasible – the son would quickly become disheartened that he is running the business and working hard for little reward.

On occasion this structure has worked where the son receives a significant salary for his efforts, the profits then being equally shared among the four children. Or the son could receive a larger proportion of the profits because he is running the business operation.

It can however often be detrimental in that all children are joined at the hip in respect to a business where only one child actively works in the business and the son is not free to paddle his own canoe, in that he may have to defer some decisions and profits to his siblings who have no involvement in the business whatsoever.

If you do operate a business where one or more of your children actively works in the business while other children do not, I would encourage you to carefully lay all of your cards on the table and have a look at the other assets that you own aside from your business. This could be property, shares, cash, superannuation, or other assets of substance. Is there a prospect that you have adequate assets aside from your business which allow your son to paddle his own canoe in the business and your remaining children each receive assets equivalent to the value of your business?

If your business is hugely successful and you don't have sufficient assets outside of your business for your remaining children to receive an equivalent value, then perhaps you can provide your son with the first option to purchase the business. A business valuation would need to be undertaken as discussed earlier and provided to your son, and he can then determine if he would like to acquire your business. You may even wish for your son to receive a discount on the valuation price as recognition for his time spent in the business and the growth of the business as a result of his knowledge and expertise. This discount can be as small or big as you feel is fair.

On other occasions, particularly where the business operations are not of significant substance, I have acted for clients who are happy to leave the business to the child who has worked in the business as a goodwill gesture. They have believed that child has assisted to grow the business, and that as a reward for their efforts the business would be left to them.

When looking at succession planning in respect to family businesses, one also needs to consider where the family business operates. If it is a farm and parts or sections will be transferred to specific beneficiaries, then there may be stamp duty and capital gains considerations. Likewise, if the business has operated from a factory for the last thirty years that is owned by the parent's Self-Managed Superannuation Fund or Family Trust, one would assume that it would be prudent for the business to continue to operate from these premises at the time of the death of the parents. The issue then becomes, who is to inherit these premises? In an ideal world it would be best for the child running the business to receive this property, but again it goes back to the issue of, are there enough other assets of the estate to compensate the remaining children who are not involved in the business?

Again, if there are not enough assets to be paid to the remaining children you may determine that the child who operates the business may have first option to acquire the property. A valuation methodology would again need to be stipulated to determine the market price for the property. Or alternatively you may determine that all your children are to own this property as joint tenants and the business would have to pay market rent.

It is important to carefully looked at how the business is held. Is it a personal asset, does it operate in a company, a trust or a Unit Trust? These are important considerations that you need to get right when putting your Estate Plan in place, as you need to ensure that correct shares or units are being transferred to the correct beneficiaries in respect to the smooth transfer of your business assets upon your death.

Some families elect to put a Memorandum of Understanding or a Deed of Family Arrangement in place between all family members. This is a document that clearly stipulates what is to happen to your estate, including business assets, and by signing the document each party confirms they clearly understand what your intentions are.

INVOLVING YOUR ADVISORS

Involving your trusted advisors – such as your accountant, financial planner and estate planning lawyer – in the succession plans of a family business will ensure that all components of your succession planning are thoroughly considered and documented correctly.

Most of you are likely to have worked extremely hard to build up your successful family business – long hours, sacrifices and damn hard work. The last thing you would want to happen is for that hard work to be diminished upon your death as a result of family conflict because you did not have a succession plan in place. I can't impress highly enough the importance of being transparent with all family members; let them know what your intentions are in respect to your family business so that there are no surprises or disconnections upon your demise.

Families can be torn apart by parents not documenting their legacy in respect to family businesses, and that is the last thing you would want to happen, particularly if you currently have a tight family unit. Implement the processes for your family business to continue and be celebrated for many years to come by the next generation. It's a nice legacy to leave behind.

Your story is the greatest legacy that you will leave to your friends, it's the longest lasting legacy you will leave to your heirs.

Steve Saint

Chapter eleven

The blended mix

Blended families are increasingly prevalent today, whether as a consequence of the death of your previous partner or a relationship breakdown. Accordingly, this can add a degree of complexity to your estate planning, especially if you own joint assets that you may wish to go to your respective children from previous relationships.

THE BASICS

Let us start with the basics. Anything that is jointly owned with your spouse automatically goes to the surviving spouse at the time of your death, as discussed in chapter five. So, if you and your spouse have a joint bank account the funds in this account pass to your spouse upon your death. If you and your spouse own property together as joint proprietors, it will pass to your spouse upon your death.

If, however, you owned property as tenants in common with your spouse, your equity in the property is an individual asset and you may make provision in your will for what you would like to happen to your equity in this property.

Often people in blended relationships purchase an initial property without consideration of how it impacts their Estate Plan and the legacy that they wish to leave behind. It is not until they go to put their Estate Plan in place that they realise the ramifications of owning property as joint proprietors as opposed to tenants in common.

You may be happy to leave all your assets to your spouse at the time of your death and have no interest in leaving any assets to your children and other family members from previous relationships. In this case, it is relatively simple to document your wishes and provisions can be made to leave all your assets that you personally own to your spouse at the time of your death.

In most cases, people in second (or third or fourth) marriages have a preference that their children from previous relationships receive all or some of their assets at the time of their death. In such instances, it's important to do an analysis of what assets you and your spouse each own and control and the manner in which they are held.

If you have purchased your residence as joint proprietors with your spouse and you wish for your equity in the property to be reflected by the amount that you contributed to the purchase then the manner in which you hold this property can be changed to tenants in common. This may be in equal shares or unequal shares depending on how much each party contributed to the property.

By instigating this strategy and owning the property as tenants in common you and your spouse may then stipulate in your individual Wills what you would like to happen to your equity in this property at the time of your death.

You may determine that you would like your spouse to have the option to reside in this property for the remainder of their life, and then subsequent to their death your equity in the property would be paid to your children. In this case, you may make provision in your Will to provide your spouse with a Life Interest in the property or a Right to Occupy the property.

This will allow your spouse to remain in the property for the remainder of their life if they so wish, provided they maintain the property and pay the applicable rates and insurances. At the time of the death of your spouse the property would be sold and your equity in the property after the payment of the applicable expenses would be paid to your children in accordance with the provisions of your Will.

There may come a time where your spouse would like to downsize from the residence or move to an alternate property, particularly as they get older and the garden and maintenance of your current property may no longer be feasible for them to manage. As an extension of this Life Interest or Right to Occupy the property, you may also consider making provision in your Will that your spouse may sell your current residence and purchase a substitute residence.

This substituted residence would be purchased and held in the same manner as your current residence, as Tenants in Common in Equal Shares with your spouse holding half the shares in the property and your executor holding the remaining half of the shares in the property in their capacity as the Legal Personal Representative of your estate.

Your executor would be responsible for overseeing the implementation and continuation of this life interest or right to occupy and ensuring that the surviving spouse is adhering to the provisions contained within this clause of your Will, by ensuring the property is well maintained and insurances are current and rates paid. If the surviving spouse wished to sell the property to downsize, they would advise your executor of this, who would then facilitate arranging the sale of your current residence and the purchase of the substitute residence.

In some instances a spouse may want to leave a sum of money for the surviving spouse at the time of their death, in which they would receive the benefit from any income during their lifetime and at the time of the death of the surviving spouse this money would revert back to the initial spouse's estate and be paid to their children. For example, you may determine to leave a sum of five hundred thousand dollars in a Capital Protective Trust for the benefit of your spouse. The Capital Protective Trust would be established in accordance with the provisions of your Will and your executor would be the trustee of the trust. The provisions of the Capital Protective Trust could stipulate that your spouse is to receive the benefit of all of the income derived from the funds held in the Capital Protective Trust during their lifetime, however they could not access any of the capital of the Trust. Upon your spouse's death the capital of this trust, which will always remain five hundred thousand dollars, will be paid to your children in accordance with the provision of your Will.

Given the role that your executor undertakes in overseeing the implementation and operation of the life interest or right to occupy and the Capital Protective Trust, it is prudent that the executor is someone who can have a working relationship with your spouse in respect to this matter. It would not, for instance, be ideal to appoint a son who despises his stepmother to undertake this role, as although the executor has a strong fiduciary duty to carry out his role in accordance with the provisions of his father's wishes, it would probably make for an extremely frustrating and uncomfortable relationship.

The Life Interest, Right to Occupy and Capital Protective Trust are valuable strategies that can be instigated in circumstances where the parties putting their Wills in place have previously been married and have children from a previous relationship. They achieve the objective of each party having use of the deceased spouse's assets during their lifetime and then upon the death of both, their respective assets end up with their own individual children and families from previous relationships.

In some instances, you and your current spouse may have children from your current relationship in addition to children from your previous relationships. The strategies detailed in the previous paragraphs can also be applied to accommodate your mutual children from your current relationship.

Your personal assets may extend beyond your residence and cash and you may have other property interests, a share portfolio or other assets that you may determine to be paid directly to your children at the time of your death. In essence this would mean your spouse would have the use of some of your assets upon your demise and your children would also receive an entitlement of other assets from your estate at the time of your death.

Another strategy that can be instigated for those with family members from a previous relationship are Mutual Wills Agreements. In this instance you and your spouse put in place your respective Wills in accordance with your wishes. In addition to putting your Wills in place you both also put in place a Mutual Wills Agreement. This agreement provides an undertaking to each other that you will not change your current Will or put in place a new Will without the consent of the other, and if your spouse has passed away, without the consent of your spouse's executor.

The strategies discussed in this chapter are just some of the strategies that can be implemented in respect to blended families. Like anyone putting in place an estate plan, your assets need to be looked at closely and if there are trusts, businesses and other complex strategies it is expedient to collectively have your accountant, financial advisor and estate planning lawyer involved in the process to ensure that all considerations of your estate plan are adequately covered.

NOT LEAVING ANYTHING TO YOUR SPOUSE

During my career as a lawyer I have had a number of clients in second marriages who both have their own financial means and do not intend to leave any bequeaths or provisions to the surviving spouse at the time of their death, preferring their assets to go straight to their children or other family members as the case may be.

This is perfectly fine. I would however recommend that a relevant clause is inserted in your Will stipulating definitively that you have not made any provision in your Will for your spouse and your reasons for doing so. This could mean an explanation along the lines of, 'I have not made any provision in my Will for my husband as he has his own financial means and it is my wish that my assets pass to my children from my previous relationship'.

A gentle word of warning: Wills for parties in a blended relationship should not be written via a Will kit from the post office. Wills pertaining to those in a blended relationship contain a level of complexity where the drafting of such Wills really needs to be undertaken by an estate planning lawyer proficient in the strategies that need to be instigated, such as the above.

This is particularly the case where family relationships may not be too strong. One of the unfavourable aspects of being a lawyer is that I see what happens to family dynamics when a stepmother or stepfather dies. It is not always pretty, particularly if the children of the deceased's spouse have not had a harmonious relationship with their stepparent. If they did not like them when their parent was alive, it is highly unlikely that they will like them when their parent is gone.

It is for this reason that it is imperative that those in a blended relationship ensure they have a well-drafted Will in place. If the Will is not well drafted and is not clear in its intention of what the testator's wishes are then it could be open for interpretation and a challenge could be brought against the estate by one of the relevant parties to the Will.

Blended relationships and families present challenges when putting in place your Estate Plan, however with the right advice and the implementation of the correct strategies you can achieve what you wish to happen to your assets in the event that you are no longer here, whether that is allowing your spouse to have the benefit of such assets during your lifetime or a combination of both your spouse having the benefit of some assets and your children receiving your remaining assets upon your demise.

You can't leave a
footprint that lasts if
you are always
walking on tip toe.

Marion Blakey

Chapter twelve

Get your super right

Superannuation is an interesting little facet of an Estate Plan. What most people do not realise is that superannuation is not automatically part of your Will, the reason being that it is not a personal asset like your cash in your bank or shares that you own in your own name. Superannuation is held on trust for you by the trustee of your superannuation fund, so at the time of your death your superannuation is a trust asset, not a personal asset.

As a consequence of this you need to ensure that you put in place a death nomination providing a direction to the trustee of your superannuation fund as to what you would like to happen to your superannuation at the time of your death. The most common nominations that you can put in place are:

- **Non-binding nomination:** this provides a nomination to the trustee in respect to where you would like your superannuation to be paid but it does not bind the trustee and they have the discretion in respect to where your superannuation death benefits are to be paid. In most cases this nomination needs to be reviewed and renewed every three years otherwise it lapses, and it is deemed that you do not have a valid nomination in place.
- **Binding death nomination:** this provides a nomination to the trustee in respect to where you would like your superannuation

to be paid and is binding on the trustee. In most cases this nomination needs to be reviewed and renewed every three years otherwise it lapses, and it is deemed that you do not have a valid nomination in place.

- **Non-lapsing binding death nomination:** this provides a nomination to the trustee in respect to where you would like your superannuation to be paid and is binding on the trustee. This nomination is in place in perpetuity or until such time that you determine to change it and it does not have to be renewed every three years.

The most common nominations are binding death nominations and non-lapsing binding nominations. The reason for this is that the trustee is bound to follow such nominations and must pay your superannuation in the manner that you have stipulated in such a nomination.

It is entirely up to you where you pay your superannuation upon your death. This would most likely depend on the structure of your family unit. In most cases a wife and husband leave their superannuation to each other. If there is no partner they may leave it directly to their children, particularly where the children are minors, or request that such superannuation death benefits are paid to their estate to be dealt with in accordance with the provisions of their Will.

If the children are adults it is often more practical to have the superannuation paid to your estate as there potentially will be less tax payable on particular components of your superannuation by having it paid to your estate rather than your children individually.

One of the frustrations of many superannuation funds is that they do not allow you to default to a reserve beneficiary if your spouse dies with you.

When putting in place your death benefit nomination it is prudent to obtain the advice of your financial advisor and lawyer to ensure that your nomination considers your investment strategy as well as your Estate Plan.

By way of example, if you are establishing a Testamentary Trust for the benefit of your children or grandchildren in accordance with the provisions of your Will, you would not wish for your superannuation to be paid directly to your children as they would not be afforded the benefits of such funds being paid to their trust.

Likewise, your financial planner may have spent many years working with you to establish the appropriate strategies for you and may have made provision for a reversionary pension to be put in place between spouses. So, in the event of the death of either of you, your superannuation death benefits would revert to the survivor of you.

Obtaining the advice of your financial advisor and estate planning lawyer will also allow you to be briefed on the tax implications of paying superannuation to certain individuals. In the event that your superannuation is paid to a spouse, children under the age of twenty-five years who are dependants or your disabled child, there would be no tax implications in respect to this payment.

There are also other instances where there may be no tax implications in respect to the payment of your superannuation, and your financial advisor will be able to advise you accordingly once they have carefully considered your individual family circumstances.

WHAT HAPPENS IF YOU DO NOT HAVE A NOMINATION IN PLACE?

So, what happens if you do not have a nomination in respect to your superannuation in place? It's a very good question, and one that more people need to be aware of. If you die without a current, valid nomination in place then it is up to the discretion of the trustee of your superannuation in respect to where your superannuation will be paid.

The trustee of your superannuation fund will need to adhere to the provisions of the fund's Trust Deed in determining where to pay your superannuation in such instances. In most cases, the Trust Deed will stipulate that your superannuation is to be paid to a dependant, being a spouse, de facto partner or minor child. In the absence of any dependants then in most cases your superannuation would be paid to your estate and distributed in accordance with your Will, should you have one in place. If no Will is in place, then it will be distributed in accordance with the intestacy provisions determined by the government. Alternatively, the Trustee of your superannuation fund may determine to pay your superannuation directly to your adult children.

Superannuation is often a vehicle that people do not give much consideration to – it is ticking over in the background for when they are older. This is why often when people separate from a partner they forget to update their binding death nomination. As a result of this I have witnessed many instances where the estranged partner of a deceased has received the deceased's superannuation because they are either listed on the binding death nomination, or are still considered a dependant given that a property settlement has not yet taken place between the deceased and their estranged partner.

In another instance, a woman who was in a relationship with her partner for six weeks successfully applied for and received her partner's superannuation upon his death. Despite not living with her partner and despite the short period of time that they were in a relationship, the trustee of the superannuation fund determined that she was a dependant and was entitled to receive her partner's superannuation death benefits. His parents and siblings were devastated by the decision as they had argued that they were entitled to such payment.

To many people superannuation may be their largest asset after property assets, and as such it needs to be given comprehensive consideration when putting an Estate Plan in place. With the right financial and legal advice, you will be able to devise and instigate a number of strategies that will protect your family and also be extremely tax effective.

Your legacy is being
written by yourself.
Make the right decisions.

Gary Vaynerchuk

Chapter thirteen

The insurance conundrum

I am not, nor do I purport to be, a financial planner or insurance broker, however I do know that insurance can be a very powerful tool in taking care of families and loved ones left behind, and as such insurance is an aspect that is increasingly becoming of value when putting an Estate Plan in place.

Putting your Estate Plan in place provides an opportunity for you to review your current insurances to check whether they are adequate for your current circumstances. Those of you who have a financial advisor would most likely go through this process on a regular basis as part of their service offering.

TOTAL PERMANENT DISABILITY INSURANCE

There are a number of different insurances that should be taken into consideration, inclusive of total permanent disability insurance. It's important to realistically sit back and ask yourself if something happened to you and you became permanently disabled, will you have adequate funds for your care and living expenses and to care and provide for your family if need be? Will your outstanding liabilities, such as home loans, be able to be serviced or paid out?

Many people go through life on autopilot, compartmentalising their journey into life and death and not giving consideration to the prospect that there could be a period of their life, whether a short period or a substantial period, where they may be incapacitated. As such, they do not plan for this period. I like to use the analogy of motor vehicle insurance; you do not take out motor vehicle insurance with the aim of running into the first car you see on the road, although some of us at some point feel very inclined to do so from time to time when cut off by other road users. Rather, motor vehicle insurance is put in place *just in case* you have the misfortune of having an accident.

The same applies for total permanent disability insurance; it is put in place just in case you become permanently disabled, whether by accident, illness or other means. Having such insurance in place will invariably take financial pressure off yourself, your family and those who would be entrusted with making decisions about your care if you were no longer in the position to make such decisions yourself.

LIFE INSURANCE

Life insurance can also be a useful tool to look after your family when you are no longer here, and can be used in a number of ways depending on your circumstances at the time of putting your Will in place.

One motivating factor for many people putting life insurance in place is to cover their children's future education costs, mortgages, debts and living expenses. When looking at these liabilities and expenses, it is ideal to look at them from a perspective that if you were not here tomorrow, how much insurance would you need to cover these debts and other costs? It is important to analyse what these costs would be. If you intend to send your children to a private school, what are the yearly school fees and additional expenses, adjusted for inflation? How much would you need to raise your children each year, and what are the associated living costs for your family? What are the outstanding loan amounts payable on mortgages, car loans, credit cards and any other liabilities?

FAMILY DYNAMICS

It's important to also look at the family dynamics. If one partner goes off to work every day and is the main breadwinner in the family, while the other partner looks after young children and is responsible for running the household, this is crucial to note when determining the amount of insurance you require.

Let us expand on this further. The partner who has the responsibility of maintaining and running the household dies. Instantaneously their role as the cook, cleaner, nanny, children's uber driver, ironing person, therapist, school canteen helper, school library and classroom helper is gone. Who then will fulfil these multiple roles? Who will ensure that your children wake up each day and are fed and dressed ready for school? Who will take them to school, collect them from school and take them to the array of after-school activities that seem to populate their afternoon schedules these days? Who will then take them home and ensure that they complete their homework, that they are fed and feel a sense of security as they are tucked away in bed for the evening?

You may be fortunate in that you have close family or friends who could step in and help you out, particularly in the initial stages. But are the initial stages sustainable long term, and what if you do not have close family or friends who would be able to come to the aid of the surviving partner if something happened to either of you? What if they had to do their full-time job and all of the above?

By looking closely at what it would effectively cost to run your household if something happened to you, it would allow you to effectively determine an insurance amount that you feel comfortable with that would help you maintain your status quo. Obtaining insurance in this amount would allow the surviving partner to obtain the services of a nanny if required, or a housekeeper, cleaner or someone to assist with the ironing.

Having such insurance proceeds would allow you the financial freedom to engage the services you may require to keep your family unit running smoothly after the loss of a partner. It would also allow you the financial security of paying off or substantially mitigating mortgages and other liabilities.

At the other end of the scale, you may have held life insurance policies for many years, primarily to pay your children's private education and to service the high level of debt that many people carry during particular times of their lives. However, you may have come out the other side, your children have completed or are almost finished their education, the mortgage has been paid out or only a nominal amount is owed, and in such instances it may no longer be necessary to carry the high level of insurance that you have held over the preceding years. A review of your circumstances may determine that it would be more viable to reduce the amount of life insurance you carry, or perhaps eliminate it altogether if your personal and financial circumstances confirm that it is no longer required.

I am often surprised by the number of clients who are unaware that they may already hold insurance as part of their superannuation. It is common for industry superannuation funds such as CBUS and Host Plus to offer insurance as part of their superannuation offerings. Depending on your age and eligibility criteria, these funds offer Death only or Death and Total Permanent Disability insurance for their members. Generally speaking, the younger you are at the time of your death or the time that you become permanently incapacitated, the higher the life insurance or TPD payment is. Such insurance payments gradually decrease in correlation to you aging. If you were not aware of such cover that may be automatically offered by your superannuation fund, perhaps check out your superannuation fund's website for further information, or even better contact them directly for clarification in respect to your insurance cover.

Recently, I acted for a client who died leaving less than two thousand dollars in his own name. He was a simple man with simple needs. He had however been in stable employment throughout his forty-plus years of life and at the time of his death the cumulative balance in his superannuation and life insurance was one million two hundred dollars, the majority of this made up of insurance. For a simple man, his beneficiaries received an almighty surprise with the amount that they received upon his death because of this very significant life insurance policy.

People sometimes say that they are not worth much, but when you take into consideration the story in the previous paragraph, you could be leaving behind more than you realise when you are no longer here and your insurances are paid out.

Insurance and blended families

Insurance has also been used as a tool by those who may have blended families. Let us say that you have young children with your current partner and you also have adult children from a previous relationship. Your current assets that you own may only sustain and look after your current partner and your young children after your death.

However, it may be your wish to provide for your adult children as well, as you do not want them to miss out or feel neglected. One way that many people get around this conundrum is by putting in place an insurance policy outside of their superannuation in their own name, in which the beneficiaries of this policy will be their adult children. By implementing this people in such situations feel that they are taking care of their young family and current partner, however they are also taking care of their adult children too and leaving a legacy to all their family members.

It is important to note that life insurance is taxed differently depending on which structure it is held in. Life insurance that is held in a superannuation fund that is paid to a dependant, that being a spouse or dependent children under the age of twenty-five years, is not taxed as the recipients are considered dependants of the deceased. However, if you made a nomination leaving your superannuation and life insurance held by the superannuation fund to your adult children, there would be tax implications when it is paid to your adult children as they are not deemed to be dependants, unless you have a disabled adult child.

It is prudent to obtain the appropriate financial advice when looking at putting life insurance policies in place so that you can then make an informed decision regarding the best life insurance policy to suit your individual circumstances, where such policies should be held, and the tax implications, if any, relating to the payment of your insurance policies upon your death.

Insurance is an integral consideration when putting your Estate Plan in place. At the very least a review of your current insurance will reinforce what you currently have in place, and such a review could be the catalyst for determining whether the level of insurance that you have is sufficient or whether additional insurance is required, dependent on where you are in your life cycle and your current circumstances.

The greatest legacy we can leave our children is happy memories.

Og Mandino

Chapter fourteen

Caring for your children

To most people, their children are their most precious asset. Deciding who will care for your minor children if you are no longer here is something that a lot of people struggle with when putting their Estate Plan in place.

Provision is made within your Will for who will care for any children under the age of eighteen who you leave behind at the time of your death. If your children's other parent survives you then they will be the guardian of your children, except for in cases where they may not be involved in your children's life or for other exceptional reasons.

Choosing the right person to be your children's guardian is an important consideration – it is not something that should be decided upon lightly.

CHOOSING A GUARDIAN

There are many factors to consider when choosing the appropriate guardian. Firstly, it should be someone your children know well and have a fantastic relationship with. Shipping your children off to another state to live with and be cared for by a long-lost relative is not ideal, especially when your children have recently lost their main carer and influencer in their life.

I am an advocate for involving older children in the process of selecting who their guardian will be. The more transparent you are with your children, the easier it will be if something happens to you as they will take comfort in knowing who will care for them. It can be scary for children of any age to have such a conversation with you, as it would be difficult for them to comprehend life without you.

However, partaking in such a process is also an opportunity for your children to tell you their thought process, and the person who you may have ascertained as being ideal to care for your children may not be a person that your children want to be cared for by. These conversations will also provide you with comfort and peace of mind, knowing that your children are happy with the person who will be appointed their guardian in your Will.

In choosing guardians for children I note that many clients tend to choose a guardian whose values align with their own. I have had many clients who have chosen not to nominate siblings as their children's guardian solely because they have a different value system and are travelling a different path in life.

Often people consider listing their parents as their children's guardians in their Will without giving it due consideration. If your parents are in their sixties and your children are aged six months and two years of age, are your parents really the best option to raise your children? Are they going to want to undertake this role? They may be looking forward to the grey nomad lifestyle and hooking their caravan onto the car and heading off on that long-awaited trip around Australia. They would also be in their mid-seventies when your children are teenagers – will their health allow them to play the role of mum and dad's taxi service, transporting them to sporting events and other activities that teenagers partake in? Will they have the energy to do so?

I am also extremely cautious in generalising as I appreciate some eighty-year-olds are fitter, more energetic and living life more so than some thirty- or forty-years-olds. For this reason, I would highly recommend you consider your parents' current position and aspirations when choosing if they are the right people to be guardians of your children. Chat to them about it; they may outright say they have had enough of child rearing, and knowing their sentiments you can then look elsewhere to determine who would be the best guardian for your children.

One of my most recent clients, let us call her Claudia, is a delightful lady. In her mid-sixties, she is leading a vibrant life and still working in a role that she absolutely enjoys. She is also bringing up her nine-year-old grandson. The child's mother is still alive, however is unable to care for him, so Claudia has been his permanent carer and guardian since he was a baby. By all accounts she is doing a wonderful job and is supported by other family members to give her regular breaks from caring for her grandson, as well as allowing him to spend quality time with other family members. In Claudia's case she has got the support networks in place that work best for her and her grandson.

LIVING ARRANGEMENTS

When selecting your children's guardian, you should also give consideration to the prospective guardian's living arrangements. If they already have four children and you have three, are they really going to want to take on the care of looking after your three children too? Will they have to extend their house or purchase a new house for everyone to comfortably fit? Or perhaps the children will have to share bedrooms in the proposed guardian's current house. It's important to give in-depth consideration to the prospective guardian's family unit and living arrangements, as although they may operate well as their current family unit, three additional children to care for may provide an extremely different dynamic.

The loss of parents is a difficult time for children; their security blanket is pulled from underneath them and their sense of normality totally eradicated, their world is forever changed. It is during this unsettling period that most parents therefore want their children to have stability and comfort from those who are already a significant part of their life, whether that be extended families, friends or other loved ones. If your child is loving school, has a strong and closely connected group of friends and a wonderful sense of community around them, would sending them to the other side of the world where your sister resides so that she can be their guardian and care for them be the right thing? Or would they be better off to remain within the community that they know and where they feel supported so that they may continue to thrive?

Of course, this is all dependent on the age of your children when you pass away and whether they are strongly ingrained within their networks at the time you pass away. You may consider that a certain person may be the most ideal person to be your children's guardian when they are four years of age, but a few years later circumstances change and they are no longer the perfect person to be your children's guardian. It is for this reason that when appointing someone to be your children's guardian you should elect that person on the basis that you would not be here tomorrow. If circumstances change in five years' time and that person is no longer the best person to be your children's guardian, you should amend your Will to reflect this and appoint someone else who is best suited to be the guardian of your children at that particular time.

One of your children may be over the age of eighteen years and you may consider appointing them as the guardian of your younger children. In determining if your elder child is the right person to be the guardian of their younger sibling or siblings, you need to give consideration to the maturity of the elder child and also whether the siblings in fact get along and have a good relationship. Is the elder sibling strong enough to be the guardian or will they be persuaded by their younger siblings? This will diminish strong decision making and potentially lead to unfavourable decisions being made in respect to your children. Is there adequate support from other family members and family friends to assist your child with raising their siblings, and additionally who can they seek guidance from if required?

When appointing someone as the guardian of your children you should have a chat with them and ask them whether they would be happy to take on this role if anything happened to you. By that I do not mean you ask them to be the guardian of your children, they say yes, and then you high-five each other and the matter is resolved. I am talking about having a really thorough chat with the proposed guardian – and I mean *really* talk – and make sure they are listening to what you are verbalising, that they clearly understand what you are saying. Ask them if they understand the implications of looking after your children, discuss their living arrangements and how this would impact their lives if your children were in their care. Are they comfortable with the drastic change having an additional child or children will bring? Do they fully comprehend what these changes will be, particularly in the initial stages when your children integrate into their family unit?

If their children go to a public school and you intend for your children to go to a private school, how do they feel about that? Do they feel comfortable with this, or will it create some division among the children? Chat with them about the rituals that you would like them to continue – would they be happy for your children to continue to partake in these rituals?

Would they be happy to accommodate your wishes of them spending time with family members, friends and loved ones so that they can retain these solid relationships?

These are conversations that allow both parties to fully understand the role of guardian and to fully comprehend each other's expectations. It will hopefully result in both parties being comfortable and a guardian being selected to care for your children if the need arises, or you may walk away from the meeting with a view that they are not the best person to be your children's guardian. Either way, they will provide you with comfort that the right decision is made.

It may take you some time to find the right guardian for your children and that is okay. Some people instinctively know straight away who the perfect person to care for your child is and that is fantastic, however others may not have this luxury and that's okay. It's a process that may take some time but at the end of the process you should come to a decision where you are comfortable with the person who you have appointed to be your children's guardian.

When appointing a guardian, it is also important to give serious consideration to who you appoint if you are appointing more than one person. If you determined to appoint your sister and her husband as the children's guardian, is this really what you want? Let us say that your sister's marriage broke down or your sister passed away, is it then your intention that you would want your brother-in-law to be the guardian of your children? In some instances, this is the case and that is fine. However, often people appoint a married couple as their guardian without really considering what they are doing.

It's all very well and good to have conversations with your children's prospective guardian and articulate your wishes in respect to your children and how you would like them raised and the prospective guardians may have a wonderful memory and may retain some of your wishes in respect to your children. However, like most people leading busy lives these days there may be parts of the conversations that do not get stored in their memory bank for future reference.

GUIDANCE FOR GUARDIANS

For this reason alone, I am an advocate of parents sitting down and leaving notes to the children's guardians in respect to the important things they would like to document about how they would like their children raised.

In my law practice, we offer clients a document called a 'Guardian Wishes' booklet. The 'Guardian Wishes' booklet is a document that allows you to stipulate your wishes as to how you would like your children raised, and things that are of importance to you in respect to the care of your children. It includes matters like the schools you would like your children to attend, the activities you would like them to partake in, whether you would like children to spend particular holiday periods with a specific family member or friend to carry on traditions and rituals, would you like them to obtain a part-time job when they attain a certain age, and so forth?

The 'Guardian Wishes' document is not legally binding on the children's guardian but it should give them a clear indication as to what your wishes are and how you would like your children to be raised. It is an invaluable tool for the guardian, particularly if your death was unexpected. Imagine being in your children's guardian's shoes, having children placed in your care unexpectedly. A million thoughts would be running through their mind regarding what they should do, and presumably they would be thinking and rationalising what you would want them to do in each circumstance.

I like to use the analogy of an instruction manual. Most things you buy come with a manual on how the item works. The 'Guardian Wishes' document is a manual in a sense; it goes a long way in helping your children's guardian know what works and what doesn't, and what you would want to happen.

Taking a little time now to put these wishes in place can be a beautiful gift that you can leave to your children and their guardian, which will be greatly appreciated by both your children and your guardian if you are no longer here. Hopefully, this document will never be needed, but if it is you have created a legacy in taking the time to care about your children and their future and providing invaluable guidance to their guardian.

It is also ideal if your children's guardian is someone who gets along well with the executor of your Will, or at least is someone who can have a strong working relationship with your executor. If your executor and guardian do not know each other, it would be ideal to introduce them to each other – perhaps arrange for both parties to attend your home for an informal gathering to get to know each other.

Your executor is the person entrusted to look after the assets of the estate and will be the one to provide your guardian with the appropriate funds for your children to cover their education, living costs and any other associated costs that you deem the guardian may require.

Your executor and guardian would normally communicate on a regular basis in respect to your children's financial needs, and if any extraordinary financial needs were required for a particular reason your children's guardian would need to seek these from your executor. Your executor has the task of ensuring that if the assets are invested that the appropriate funds are available to pay to the children's guardian as and when required in accordance with any directions you have left to your executor.

Your guardian and executor may be one and the same person. People often ask if there is a problem having the same person in these dual roles, and I prescribe to the analogy of my previous principal when I started as a young lawyer, who often decreed, if you trust someone with the lives of your children, why would you not trust them with your money too?

The decision regarding having the same person in a dual role is a personal one for you to make. It is also worth noting that being an executor carries a strong fiduciary duty to the beneficiaries of an estate and that they must always act in the best interests of the beneficiaries. Should they not abide by these fiduciary duties the beneficiaries may then have recourse against the executors.

Most executors do the right thing by the beneficiaries. Your personal experience and relationships with the people you appoint to the role of executors and guardian should guide you in choosing whether they are the appropriate person for these respective roles.

The thought of not being here to watch our children grow and share in their journey through life, particularly when they are young, is hard to comprehend and is a thought that we often don't want to give too much contemplation to.

Taking the time to carefully consider who would care for your children if you were no longer here will however provide you with some peace of mind that you have navigated the steps and put things in place so that if the unexpected or unwanted happened to you, your children will be well looked after by the people who you want them to be looked after by in accordance with your wishes.

Your life is your message to the world. Make sure it is inspiring.

Sady Ali Khan

Chapter fifteen

Gifts to VIPs

Many of us have special sentimental items that we would like to leave to certain people (our very important people, or VIPs) when we are no longer here. If this is the case for you, it would be expedient for you to document the items that you would like to leave to specific people. This is generally done in one of two ways:

- you can specifically list each bequeath in your Will
- your Will can refer to any gift provision list that you may leave.

In the latter case you can put this list in place at any time by stipulating clearly each gift and who is to receive each item, and date and sign this list and place it with a copy of your Will. You may then update it at any time by destroying the old gift list and putting a new one in place. So in essence, if someone annoys you and you no longer want to leave them their designated gift you can easily remove the provision for their gift by putting in place a new list.

PERSONAL ITEMS

During my career, I have found that people are either advocates for a gift list or they are not. What I will say is that it is the area where I see families quibble the most when their parents are gone. The more definitive you are in distributing your personal assets to specific people the better, as it is often the little sentimental things that tear families apart rather than large monetary items that you leave behind.

Who receives mum's diamond ring is often a contentious issue, together with who is to receive grandpa's war medals, and so on. The eldest son may feel he is entitled to the war medals but the youngest son with an interest in military history may be inclined to think he should be the recipient of these medals.

I recall a case a decade or so ago where a commentator aged in his thirties died without a Will. A dispute occurred over his estate, and proceedings were initiated in the Supreme Court of Victoria over his estate, with the parties to the proceedings being the deceased's partner and his parents. The most contentious issue was not the most substantial asset of the estate, being a monetary component, but rather the most cherished possessions: sporting memorabilia and private journals.

One of the things I dislike most about being an estate planning lawyer is when clients say, 'They can sort it out between them … I will be dead and won't be here so I don't care what happens'. The reason I so despise this comment is because when you leave it to the executor to sort out which child gets what, it can create enormous tension and animosity between family members, let alone the strain and responsibility that you are placing on your executor.

Once close family relationships that took a generation or two to create can dissolve in an instant over something so simple as who gets a sentimental item that belonged to you. I implore you to think carefully about this when putting your Estate Plan in place, and keep at the forefront of your mind what sort of legacy you would like to leave behind.

I assume the most important thing for you would be that if your family were a close family unit prior to your death you would like that to be retained after your death. If so, take the time to go through the personal items that you know mean something to your loved ones and do a VIP gift list. If you are so inclined, ask them if there is anything they would like; they may really like something that you were not aware they liked.

I once acted for a dear client, a prim and proper lady in her mid-eighties, who arrived at our initial consultation to discuss her Estate Plan with a three-page list of gifts that she wanted to leave to her family and other VIPs. I vividly recall the list featured crystal, crystal, and more crystal. However, I do admire her for sitting down so diligently and taking the time to document who she would like to receive her personal belongings.

MONETARY BEQUEATHS

In addition to leaving gifts of personal belongings to VIPs, some people may wish to leave a monetary bequeath to certain people. Such monetary bequeaths are paid prior to the distribution of the balance of your estate. If you determine to leave five bequeaths of ten thousand dollars then fifty thousand dollars of your estate will be utilised in the first instance to pay these before the balance of your estate is paid to the remaining beneficiaries of your Will.

Leaving money to charity

It is also becoming more prevalent for people to leave gifts to charitable organisations, particularly if they do not have children, or as a reserve distribution in the event that all members of their immediate family pass away together. People may have a strong connection to these charities, because they have assisted family members or loved ones during their lifetime or they may resonate with the philosophies of the charity that they would like to leave a bequeath to.

When leaving bequeaths to a charity in your Will it is imperative that you list the full name of the charity, their Australian Business Number and address so that it is extremely clear which charity you wish to leave a bequeath to. With so many charities in existence today, some of which have very similar names, it is crucial that they are adequately identified so that a part of your estate does not end up with the wrong charitable organisation.

There have been occasions where the executor or trustee of an estate has been found to have paid bequeaths to a charity to which it was not the deceased's intention to leave a bequeath, purely because the charity was not adequately identified and was confused with a charity with a similar name. Several older Wills have passed my desk with bequeaths 'to the lost dog's home'. It is all very well to leave such a generous bequeath, however the contentious issue is that a quick glance on Google will identify that there are a number of lost dogs' homes. In such instances your executor may not be able to distinguish the specific charity this bequeath was intended for.

In addition, when leaving charitable bequeaths you may wish to stipulate whether the bequeath is to be used for the charity's general purposes or if there is a specific program or project that you would like these funds to be used for.

Gift lists are often overlooked when putting a Will in place. It is often nice for your children and other loved ones to receive a specific gift from you upon your death, no matter what the monetary value of this sentimental item is. Leaving a gift list may also alleviate future conflict between relevant parties when you are no longer here, particularly if there is already some element of friction within your family and in cases where some of your children do not get on well with each other.

The things you do for yourself are gone when you are gone, but the things you do for others remain as your legacy.

Kalu Ndukwe Kalu

Chapter sixteen

Who will receive your legacy?

The answer to this question will very much be dependent upon your family structure, where you are in your life cycle, you own values and choices. There is no right or wrong for who you leave your estate to; most people leave it to those they love.

Others leave it to those who have helped and supported them through their lifetime.

In deciding who to leave your assets to you need to know where all your assets live. What assets do you own personally, what assets do you own jointly and what assets do you control? The importance of each category of assets was expanded on in chapter six of this book. Upon reading this chapter you will note that you can make provisions for some classes of assets in your Will, however other classes of assets have different mechanisms that are required to be put in place.

In my practice, where there is a family with a couple and children with no blended marriage, it is common to leave assets to each other and then to the children and grandchildren, in that order.

WHOLE FAMILY DYING AT ONCE

One contentious issue that some people overlook when putting a Will in place is, who would receive your estate if your immediate family died together? People often put in place a Will where if a spouse passes it goes to the surviving spouse, and if the surviving spouse passes it goes to the children. But what would happen if all of you were in a motor vehicle accident together and you all died together? These events are not an everyday occurrence, however it is important to make provision in your Will in respect to who would be your reserve beneficiaries and receive your assets in this instance. None of us have a crystal ball; we do not know when our time is up, so we need to make provisions for every possible eventuality.

If you are in a blended marriage you may want your partner to receive your assets at the time of your death, which is perfectly fine. An extension of this is you may have an expectation that upon your partner's death they will leave the assets that you left to your partner to your children. The reality of the situation is that once your assets pass to your partner they are free to do with those assets as they see fit and are not obliged to put a Will in place leaving such assets to your children. The exception to this is where you and your spouse put in place Mutual Wills during your lifetime.

It is becoming increasingly common for couples in a blended marriage to leave the surviving partner use of their assets during their lifetime, with these assets to pass to their own children upon the death of the surviving partner. The strategies that can be implemented to achieve this are discussed further in chapter eleven, The Blended Mix.

AT WHAT AGE CAN CHILDREN ACCESS THEIR INHERITANCE?

One contentious issue that seems to frequently arise is, at what age would you like your children to receive their inheritance? This is particularly relevant when leaving an inheritance to children under the age of eighteen years – it is important to stipulate in your Will at what age you would like them to receive this inheritance. The age could be a sticking point for many parents, as they don't want their children to receive their inheritance when they are too young, but at the same time, they do not want to be seen to be 'ruling from the grave'.

A former colleague of mine received an inheritance of half a million dollars from his grandfather at age twenty-one, and over the next two years he had the time of his life, spending his inheritance on travel, parties and an array of things he didn't really need, until he was back where he started: flat broke. He received a further inheritance at age thirty and invested this money in property. He still lives in that home today, mortgage free, and is so grateful he learned his lesson the first time around and learned the value of money, so that when the second inheritance came he treated it with the respect and gratitude it deserved.

In 2002, Melbourne was shocked by the brutal and senseless murder of socialite Margaret Wales-King and her husband Paul King. The media interest in this case was intense: why would anyone want to murder a wealthy older couple living a relatively normal existence? Margaret Wales-King's son, Matthew, was hastily viewed as a suspect, particularly given he did not do a particularly efficient job of covering his tracks, and he was subsequently convicted of both the murder of his mother and stepfather and sentenced to thirty years in jail. Margaret was a stylish and astute woman with wealth speculated to be around five million dollars at the time of her death.

What stood out for many who followed the daily media commentary in respect to this case is that Margaret Wales-King left what many said was an unusual clause in her Will. She stipulated that her children were only to receive their inheritance when they attained the age of forty years. Some say that she was ruling from the grave. Margaret Wales-King is on record as saying she wanted to ensure that two generations of hard work was not wasted by the third. It is a comment that many hard-working parents would most likely subscribe to, however very few would deem it necessary to wait until their children are aged forty to receive their inheritance, preferring them to enjoy the benefit of their inheritance at a much younger age. The irony in this case is that Matthew Wales did not inherit from his mother's estate as a person who kills another cannot be deemed to benefit from the crime. His siblings however agreed to award his young son $200,000 from Margaret Wales-King's estate for ongoing maintenance, a much smaller proportion than his father would have received.

You may have several assets in your asset pool and may wish to leave specific assets to particular children. If your children are adults it may be prudent to chat with them to see if there is a particular asset that they may want to receive after your death. One of your children may have a strong sentiment for your family home or beach property, or perhaps one of your children currently lives in one of your properties and would like to continue to do so after your death.

Many parents have an idealistic view of the world and think that they should leave their assets to their children jointly at the time of their death. I have had many an occasion when clients have advised me that the family home must be retained by both of their children and they would like both of their adult children to be joint proprietors of this property subsequent to their death, and that one of them may want to move into the property.

This may be the case, and the parents may be spot on with their assumption – or so they tell me. However, frequently after meeting with me and on my advice, they have a chat with their children and find out that this is *not* what their children want at all. Neither of their children want to move into the house and neither child has a desire to own the property with their sibling.

Quite often the thought of being joined at the hip with their sibling is not a pleasant one, particularly if they are at different stages of their life, and more significantly if they do not get along all that well. Chances are, if they don't get along too well while you are alive, they are less likely to get along when you are no longer here, particularly if you were the glue that held the family unit together.

So, although you may be extremely attached to a particular property or other asset and want it retained after your death, others may not share your sentiments.

You may have family members who work in your family business or you may have a disabled child or a child who cannot control their own inheritance. Or alternatively you may wish to leave a child or other close family member out of a Will. The mechanism for making provisions in your Will in these instances is discussed in the succeeding chapters of this book.

PEOPLE WITH NO CHILDREN

I have found single people and couples without children often leave their assets to nieces and nephews who they have solid relationships with and close friends.

Recently, I assisted an executor with the probate of a cousin. She had not seen her cousin, who lived interstate, for over thirty years, however kept in regular contact by text and letters as this was his preferred way of communication – he despised speaking on the telephone. He was a single man who had never married, lived alone and to the best of the executor's knowledge lived a quiet life.

Each year the executor would send him a Christmas card and pudding to let him know she was thinking of him. The biggest surprise came upon his death when the executor received a copy of his Will. He had left everything to the executor's three children, whom he had never met. Being adult children in their thirties and forties with young children of their own, the legacy they received from a long-lost relative they had never met made a significant difference to each of their lives.

Some people decide to leave their legacy based on who needs their money the most. I have had clients who overlook family members whom they are not close to and leave their assets to close family friends or other people who have had an influence or impact on their life.

Some people like to leave specific monetary bequeaths to particular family members, including siblings and grandchildren, and others like to leave such bequeaths to close friends. These bequeaths are generally paid out before the remaining distribution of your estate to your beneficiaries.

I have also witnessed an emergence of clients leaving monetary bequeaths to charities, whether it be a charity that has assisted them or a charity that is close to their heart by way of the work they undertake. If you do leave a bequeath to a charity it is essential that you ensure that the correct charity name is listed in your Will as there a number of charities with very similar names. For more on this see chapter fifteen.

If all else fails and you can't decide who to leave your legacy to, maybe you could follow the footsteps of Portuguese aristocrat Luis Carlos de Noronha Cabral de Camara, who had no one to leave his massive estate to so he chose seventy names at random from the Lisbon phone book to leave his estate to.

Leaving a legacy will make a difference to people's lives. It will in essence be your final act, it will impact the lives of those that you leave behind and it has the ability to strengthen or destroy family relationships. Putting a legacy in place should be something you give considerable thought to. At the end of the day you and only you know what you would like to happen to your assets, and as such you should implement an Estate Plan that reflects your wishes so your legacy goes to those who you dearly want to receive it.

Legacy is not leaving something for people, it's leaving something in people.

Peter Strople

Chapter seventeen

Intergenerational Trusts

An Intergenerational Trust can make an enormous difference to the type of legacy that you leave behind, and are often the most asset protective way in which to leave your loved ones their inheritance. They are most commonly referred to as a 'blood lineage trust', and they are a trust that can be established to benefit multiple generations of family members. Commonly known and referred to these days as a Testamentary Trust, they have multiple benefits and can be an extremely powerful estate planning tool.

TESTAMENTARY TRUST WILLS ARE COMMON

Although they have been around for many years, Testamentary Trusts have often been thought to be only associated with the affluent members of society. This perception has eroded over the past decades to the point where Testamentary Trust Wills are commonplace.

In my own law practice, considering that we deal with many business owners and entrepreneurs, Testamentary Trusts are particularly highly regarded and embraced by clients when putting their Estate Plan in place.

One reason for this is that the large majority of my clients are extremely hard-working people. They are self-made, motivated people who have made the most of the opportunities that came their way as a result of their hard work and consequently reaped the financial rewards. Given the sweat, blood and tears that went into creating their wealth they are adamant that such wealth is destined to stay within their family unit upon their demise.

Testamentary Trusts have a perpetuity period of eighty years, so essentially a number of generations can receive and enjoy the benefits of the trust.

ASSET PROTECTION

With an increasing number of marriages crumbling and divorce rates soaring, you do not want your hard-earned wealth falling into the hands of one of your children's estranged partners in the event of a child's relationship breakdown. By making provision in your Will leaving your children's inheritance in a Testamentary Trust it may protect their inheritance from any divorce or family law risks if your child's relationship breaks down. On the other hand, leaving your children's inheritance to them personally exposes their inheritance to divorce proceedings.

Given the diverse world that we now live in there are a multitude of people willing to take risks to bring their business idea to fruition. I, like many others, love an innovative business idea and love to celebrate the enthusiasm and persistence in seeing people bring their idea to life. Sadly, sometimes the opposite occurs and all that is left is a pile of debt which the budding entrepreneur is personally liable to repay.

Alternatively, you may have a child who works in a high-risk occupation – a doctor, engineer, accountant, financial advisor or perhaps carrying on the role of a director. If something adverse happened during them undertaking these roles and they were sued they could be held personally liable for any actions brought upon them by the aggrieved party.

The scenarios that I have presented in the preceding two paragraphs show how your child's inheritance could clearly be exposed in these circumstances, particularly if your child was served with bankruptcy proceedings. Creditors and other associated parties could only seek recourse to monies owed by your child from them in their own personal capacity.

If your child had received their inheritance in their own name and hence the assets were now their individual assets, the creditors and other associated parties would have recourse in recovering funds owed to them. If however your child's inheritance was paid to a Testamentary Trust for their benefit at the time of your death then these assets would be held on trust for them and are not personal assets, hence the creditors and other associated parties would not have recourse in respect to these assets.

HOW MUCH MONEY DO YOU NEED?

There are different schools of thought regarding how much money is required in an estate before it is feasible to put an estate plan into place. It really depends on the client's circumstances, however I generally adopt the view that there should be minimum assets of more than five hundred thousand dollars to make the implementation of Testamentary Trusts in a Will a viable proposition.

One of the concerns that many clients have is what happens to their assets if one of them passes away and the survivor re-partners. Testamentary Trusts can be a useful tool in such cases as the assets of the deceased's partner could be paid to a Testamentary Trust for the benefit of the surviving partner and their children. These assets are then protected for this family unit, so if the surviving spouse re-partners these assets are in essence quarantined from the new partner.

Your spouse may be in a particularly high-risk occupation or carrying on a business and property could be currently held in your name for asset-protection purposes. Making provision in your Will for your spouse to receive these assets in a Testamentary Trust can protect their inheritance in the event that anything was to happen to you.

Of course, there are some limitations to this strategy, as – for instance – the main residence may currently be jointly owned by both you and your spouse, meaning that at the time of the death of you or your spouse the property automatically passes to the surviving spouse and hence would not be able to go into the Testamentary Trust.

Testamentary Trusts are created within the provisions of your Will, and depending on the provisions of your Will would sit dormant until the time of your death or the time of the death of both you and your spouse.

In some instances, there may be one or more Testamentary Trusts created in a Will. I once acted for a client who had a beachhouse which had been in their family for many years; her adult children and grandchildren often congregated at the beachhouse and together as a family they created many wonderful memories. It was her wish that this property remained for all of her children's benefit subsequent to her death, and as such a Testamentary Trust was created in her Will in which the beachhouse would be placed subsequent to her death. Her children were joint trustees and beneficiaries of this Testamentary Trust.

On other occasions, parents acknowledge that their children are not all cut from the same cloth, they have different needs and financial circumstances, so to join them at the hip by having one Testamentary Trust may not be feasible. If your children have a poor relationship with each other or one of your children's spouses, then it is most likely not going to be feasible to have a single Testamentary Trust for the benefit of all your children. Similarly, if you have children from different relationships it may be prudent for them to have separate Testamentary Trusts.

It is commonplace for clients to make provisions in their Will for separate Testamentary Trusts for each of their children; this way they may each paddle their own canoe, so to speak. Each child would be the trustee of their own Testamentary Trust and would have effective control in respect to all the assets in their Testamentary Trust.

Where a minor is a beneficiary of a Testamentary Trust created solely for them, the executor of the Will is normally appointed the trustee until such time that the minor child attains the age at which the Will stipulates that they are to receive their inheritance, at which time the executor will resign as trustee of the Testamentary Trust and the child will be appointed trustee.

There can be variations in respect to who will be the trustee of the trust, and it is at your discretion in respect to who will be the trustee of your children's Testamentary Trust.

In some instances you may have a child who cannot control their own money for a range of reasons, whether due to a disability, addiction or being a spendthrift, and in such cases you may not want your child to control their own funds. In such instances you would appoint an alternate person to be the trustee of your child's Testamentary Trust. This would mean that your child would receive the benefit from the trust, however they would not control the assets in such a trust.

Testamentary Trusts have long been highly regarded because of the favourable tax treatment, which can be of a significant benefit to your family. In particular, distributions of up to eighteen thousand dollars per year may be paid to a minor child and no tax is payable as the child is taxed at normal adult tax rates. If there were three minor children within the family unit this would amount to fifty-four thousand dollars in distributions being paid to them from the Testamentary Trust and no tax would be payable.

The concessional taxation of distributions paid to minors is beneficial not just from a perspective of your children but also your grandchildren. Essentially the Testamentary Trust that you created for the benefit of your family could pay for or assist in paying for your grandchildren's education.

If your child had to personally pay for your grandchildren's education they would firstly need to pay any tax earned on the income at the applicable marginal tax rate, which means they would be paying for your grandchildren's education with their post-tax dollars.

By comparison, if you had left your child's inheritance to them in a Testamentary Trust your grandchildren's education could be paid for or partly paid for with a tax-free income, which would be a much more favourable outcome for your family.

There have been some recent taxation amendments that relate to the generation of income from assets in a Testamentary Trust and the concessional taxation of minors, so it would be prudent to obtain the appropriate legal and financial advice in respect to the concessional taxation of income from a Testamentary Trust should you wish to put in place a Testamentary Trust Will.

Some people are of the view that Testamentary Trusts are just for those with partners and children. This is not the case at all. Testamentary Trusts can also be put in place for the benefit of other family members too. A single woman with no partner or children may determine that she would like her assets to pass to her nieces and nephews at the time of her death. In this instance she could put in place a Testamentary Trust in her Will in which each of her nieces and nephews would be the beneficiaries.

Testamentary Trusts can be a very powerful estate planning tool; one lawyer that I know refers to them as the 'Ferraris of estate planning', and I personally think that is a very appropriate reference indeed. They are powerful, and can add an element of sophistication in ensuring that your legacy goes to your beneficiaries in the best way possible.

We don't live forever ...
Our legacy does.

Greg Pitt

Chapter eighteen

Making provisions for Children who cannot control their inheritance

There is a tendency for parents to wish to leave their assets equally between their children. It is however becoming increasingly common for parents to express concern that one or more of their children does not have the ability to manage their inheritance.

There are a variety of reasons for this, the most common one being that their child has a substance or dependency issue, whether that be alcohol, drugs or otherwise. There are also common instances when parents advise that their child is just no good with money and does not understand the value of it and generally speaking spends every dollar they receive quickly.

One of my clients had a son who was a drifter who moved around quite often, depending on where he could find work. At the time of assisting my clients with putting in place their estate plan their son resided in central Australia. He came to Melbourne for a visit and had calculated that it would take three petrol tanks full to get here and three tanks for the return journey. He then put enough money aside for the six tanks of petrol and spent all the remaining money that he had received from his last pay cheque.

While in Melbourne he did some extensive day trips, which of course used more of his allocated fuel. It was not until just prior to leaving Melbourne to head home to central Australia that he realised that he did not have sufficient funds for the three tanks of petrol that he required to get home. Off to the bank of mum and dad he went to obtain the required funds for that additional tank of petrol.

Although my clients' son could function quite independently on a day-to-day basis, he had absolutely no concept of money, and my clients were extremely concerned that if he should receive a significant inheritance that it would be gone in no time at all. Their son was also very easily influenced, so they did not want their hard-earned money going to people that their son met on his travels.

With this in mind it was our clients' wish that their son received the same inheritance as his two other siblings but for such inheritance to be 'protected' in some way.

We have also had similar requests from parents of children who have significant drug or alcohol dependency issues. The last thing they want to happen is that their children's inheritance is used to feed their drug or alcohol habit. They do however express their desire that their child's inheritance is used for their benefit, to look after and provide for them during their child's lifetime.

CAPITAL PROTECTIVE TESTAMENTARY TRUSTS

One way that we can assist clients with children who are deemed not to be able to control their own inheritance is by putting in place what is called a Capital Protective Testamentary Trust. (The name of this type of trust may vary between and within jurisdictions, however for the purposes of this chapter they will be referred to as a 'Capital Protective Testamentary Trust'.)

This trust is established within the provisions of your Will and makes provision for the inheritance of the child who cannot look after their own inheritance to be paid into this trust. Your executor or another independent person will control this trust on behalf of your child. Should you wish, you may stipulate what the funds of this trust can be used for.

It could be a provision of the trust that the funds may be used to provide for accommodation for your child. This could be acquiring a property for them, or it could be for paying rent on any accommodation in which your child chooses to reside. The funds could also be used towards any rehabilitation facility that your child may attend, if required.

In addition, the funds of the trust could be used for medical expenses, medical insurance, education, expenditure on personal furnishings and fittings, recreation, entertainment, holiday travel and accommodation, as well as personal belongings.

Depending upon your child's circumstances you may also determine that they are to receive an income from the trust, payable at regular intervals. In making this provision it's also important to give consideration to the impact of such income payments for your child in the event that they are in receipt of Centrelink benefits, as this could have a detrimental effect on any such government benefits they receive.

It is therefore prudent that your executor sits down with your child on a periodic basis, whether quarterly or biannually, to determine what your child's needs are and what their requests are. Your executor should also seek the appropriate financial and tax advice on how best to invest the funds in your child's trust to meet the financial requirements of your child's needs.

The primary role of your executor in administering your child's trust in their capacity as trustee of your child's Capital Protective Testamentary Trust is to ensure that the needs and requirements are being met in accordance with your wishes and the provisions of the Capital Protective Testamentary Trust.

It is important to note that all assets in the Capital Protective Testamentary Trust are held on trust by the trustee and at no time is the capital of the trust ever held by your child in their own individual name.

Capital Protective Testamentary Trusts are the most common way to make provision for such a child's inheritance. There are however variations to this that an estate planning lawyer would be able to provide further insights about, dependent on your circumstances and those of your child.

Capital Protective Testamentary Trusts are a useful tool for parents who want all children to share their legacy equally but have concerns that one of their children cannot control their legacy themselves. By implementing a Capital Protective Trust in your Will you achieve your objective of your children being treated equally and that they will be adequately looked after.

Create your legacy
and pass the baton.

Billie Jean King

Chapter nineteen

Caring for disabled children

Caring for a severely disabled child is a lifelong journey. Your responsibilities remain the same as you get older, and a continuing consideration for those with disabled children is, who will care for their disabled child at the time of their death?

THE OPTIONS

There are several different options available, depending on your family unit, your wishes, and the wishes of your disabled child.

Historically, disabled children were often institutionalised with the state responsible for their care. This option is no longer preferrable, and these days it is much more feasible that such disabled children live cohesively within the family unit as an integral member of the family.

Throughout my career I have dealt with parents who have disabled children who they personally care for within the family home, continuing throughout adulthood. On occasion they may receive outside assistance from personal care assistants to help with such care, however they generally remain hands-on in attending to the care of their disabled child. The introduction of the National Disability Insurance Scheme has also assisted disabled children and their families in this regard.

One of the positive aspects of disabled children living with family members is that it provides them with familiarity and routine from a young age.

Some adult disabled children may elect to live in supported housing which allows them to live with other disabled adults in a supportive and communal environment where they share activities, meals and their social circle.

For those who do care for disabled children, it is ideal for you to have that all-important discussion in respect to not just who will care for your disabled child's needs on a daily basis but also what financial provision will be provided in respect to your child's care?

Some time ago I acted for clients in their seventies who had a disabled son, who we shall call Jack, who continued to reside with his parents as an adult. Jack's mother had been his primary carer during his lifetime, with his father now providing additional support upon his retirement. It was their strong wish that their family continue to care for Jack upon their death.

This sounds like a simple request, however when the family sat down for a family meeting to discuss their son's care some home truths emerged. The client's two daughters advised that while they so admired their parents' commitment, resilience and devotion to caring for Jack over such an extensive period of time, and although they loved their brother very much, they both could not provide the level of commitment that the parents had provided in caring for their brother.

Both daughters had young families of their own and extremely busy work commitments, which left them with little time to take on additional duties. They conveyed to the parents that they would be more than happy for Jack to visit them for a regular weekend stay when their family commitments allowed, but they could not undertake to care for him on a full-time basis, even with assistance.

Jack's parents were devastated to learn of their daughters' sentiments, as they had always assumed that one of their daughters would undertake the role of Jack's carer subsequent to their death. This story emphasises the importance of having family discussions and not merely assuming what will happen. Without having the family discussion, Jack's parents would have been none the wiser in respect to his sisters' sentiments relating to Jack's ongoing care.

The family discussions gave Jack's parents a reality check, and prompted them to look at other options in respect to Jack's care. Shortly after, Jack spent a period of time in a supported living environment, and given it was his first time living away from his family it went remarkably well, and by all accounts Jack enjoyed interacting with his newfound friends away from his family unit.

Most importantly, this exercise gave Jack's parents peace of mind and comfort in knowing that although Jack would not live in a full-time capacity with his siblings subsequent to their passing, there were other options available to him which Jack had enjoyed and was adaptable to.

The key takeaway when discussing the future needs and care of your disabled child is to discuss it openly and transparently with all relevant parties, let your disabled child tell you what they would like to happen, let your other children provide their perspective, and hopefully within the mix there is some positive resolution that is beneficial to all parties.

Over my career as a lawyer, I have also acted for numerous clients with a disabled child where one of their other children has willingly offered to care for their disabled sibling when their parents are no longer alive. Some even adequately plan for this eventuality when buying or building a home by ensuring there are self-contained quarters for their sibling, where they will have their own space but still be part of the family unit.

Once the issue of where your disabled child will live has been decided, you then need to focus on how they will be looked after financially.

SPECIAL DISABILITY TRUSTS

One of the most popular options available to parents with a disabled child is a Special Disability Trust. A Special Disability Trust allows a disabled child to benefit from the assets of the trust without having control of the assets contained in the trust. Essentially, it is a mechanism for parents or other immediate family members to plan and provide for the care, accommodation, medical costs and other needs of a child with a severe disability during their lifetime.

One of the favourable aspects of the Special Disability Trust is that the assessable assets of the Special Disability Trust up to $694,000 (indexed on 1 July each year) are exempt from the Centrelink assets test. In addition, your family home, which is deemed to be a principal place of residence, is not an assessable asset and is not included in the asset value limit. So if you for whatever reason determined to leave your residence to your disabled child it would not be included in the asset value limit for Centrelink purposes.

In addition, income or distributions received from a Special Disability Trust by your disabled child are not assessable under the Centrelink income test.

As the purpose of the Special Disability Trust is to provide for the care and accommodation needs of your disabled child, withdrawals from the trust are limited to withdrawals in respect to care and accommodation needs together with an amount up to $12,500 (as at 1 July 2020) for discretionary spending. Such discretionary spending can include household items, recreation and leisure, clothing, and social inclusion workshops.

These favourable Centrelink considerations have been appealing to many parents of disabled children and are one reason why such trusts are often implemented in looking after the future financial needs of disabled children.

In order to put a Special Disability Trust in place for the benefit of your disabled child there are a number of requirements that must be met. Amongst these requirements is that your child has a severe disability, which includes a severe physical, intellectual, psychiatric, or behavioural disability or medical condition.

Other requirements of the Special Disability Trust are:

- the primary purpose must be to provide for the care and accommodation needs of your disabled child
- an independent trustee must be appointed
- the Special Disability Trust must comply with prescribed investment restrictions and provide annual financial statements.

The Special Disability Trust must also have a Model Trust Deed which contains the appropriate clauses required for the trust to be classified as a Special Disability Trust Deed.

The Special Disability Trust can be put in place in accordance with the provisions of your Will or it may be established by a Model Trust Deed prior to your death. If it is established in accordance with the provisions of your Will, the amount to be paid to the Special Disability Trust will also be stipulated in your Will. Upon your death the Special Disability Trust will be established for your disabled child and the nominated funds paid to the Special Disability Trust for the benefit of your disabled child.

The trustee, who will be appointed by you, will be entrusted to look after the funds in the Special Disability Trust on behalf of your disabled child. This may be one of your children, a relative, family friend or any other person that you trust to control and manage the assets on behalf of your disabled child. It should be someone who knows your disabled child well and aligns with your values and understands the needs of your disabled child, and who has the best interests and welfare of your disabled child at heart. Your trustee should also be someone who is receptive and proactive to seeking financial and legal advice.

A Special Disability Trust can provide fantastic benefits, however it is imperative that the appropriate legal and financial advice is obtained prior to the establishment of a Special Disability Trust for the benefit of your disabled child.

There are other options available in respect to making provisions for a disabled child in your Will; this book predominantly focuses on the most popular option, being the Special Disability Trust. I acknowledge however not all disabled children will meet the requirements of having a severe disability for the purposes of the implementation of a Special Disability Trust. An estate planning lawyer would be able to advise you of alternate options available to you depending on your circumstances and depending on the severity of your child's disability.

HOW MUCH TO LEAVE TO A DISABLED CHILD?

The question of how much of your estate to leave to a disabled child is a challenging one for parents. If the disabled child is an only child, it is usually a non-issue with the whole of the inheritance going to the disabled child. However, if you do have other children in addition to your disabled child, it can present a conundrum in respect to how to divide your estate fairly between your disabled child and other members of your family. Some parents follow the equality model and determine that each child should be treated equally and as such receive an equal share of their estate.

Others may leave a greater share to a disabled child as they feel they may have more need for funds some time in the future. Some parents take a different approach and leave a greater amount to non-disabled children, believing that their disabled child will receive funds from the public purse to assist their needs.

There is no right or wrong amount to leave a disabled child or any other child, it is very much a personal decision and one that you need to give some considered thought to. It is likely no one knows your family unit better than you and no one knows the needs, hopes and aspirations of each family member like you do. I do know that once you have made provisions in your estate plan for your disabled child and indeed all other members of your family whom you wish to make provisions for that you will have a considerable level of comfort knowing that you have made provisions for their care, wellbeing and future.

I’ve learned that people will forget what you said, people will forget what you did, but people will never forget how you made them feel.

Maya Angelou

Chapter twenty

Leaving someone out of your Will

No family is perfect. Many of us have skeletons in our closet, and to many the Hollywood movies of everyone playing happy families are extremely superficial. The cold hard fact is that many family members do not like each other.

ESTRANGED CHILDREN

It is becoming increasingly common for clients in my law practice to advise that they want to leave a child out of their Will. Often they have been estranged from this child for a number of years and do not have a meaningful relationship with them. They see no prospect of reconciliation with that child during their lifetime – they have removed them from their life and do not wish for them to receive any inheritance at the time of their death.

In other instances, some people choose not to leave an inheritance to one of their children because that child has independently through their own hard work accumulated their own assets and financial security, and so they deem that child does not need to receive an inheritance as they have their own financial means. In such cases, they may leave that child's inheritance to that child's children, believing that the specific family unit is still obtaining a benefit, just not the parent of the children who receive a benefit. Or alternatively, they may leave that particular child's family unit out of their Will all together.

Some people also disinherit children because their children show very little interest in them or spend very little time with them. This can result in the parent feeling unloved, and as a result they may be inclined to leave their inheritance to their remaining children who do show them interest and spend time with them.

I encourage anyone who intends to leave a child or other family member out of a Will to consider this omission very carefully. Think of it from the perspective of the person who you are intending to leave out. If it is a child, think of how they will feel if they are left out of a Will. In no way am I attempting to discourage you from leaving a child or other beneficiary out of a Will; I am just suggesting that you think your decision through carefully as it could have significant ramifications. That being said, your assets are your assets, so you should feel inclined to leave them to whomever you wish to leave them to.

It can be devastating to be left out of a Will. I have a close friend I have known for over thirty years whose grandmother died last year. The grandmother lived in a different state to my friend, and her parents also spent considerable time in that state caring and checking in on the grandmother. My friend and family were constantly by the grandmother's side for the last six weeks of her life. Imagine their shock when upon her death they found out that the grandmother's Will left everything solely to her daughter and absolutely nothing to her son, my friend's father. Nothing. This was a lady who had spent numerous hours and family occasions in the company of my friend's family and had given the impression of a loving, civilised family unit, only to leave her son nothing. In addition, there was no mention in the Will as to why she had omitted her son or why she had failed to acknowledge him in her Will.

The reality for his omission comes down to one simple consideration. He was an extremely successful businessman who had climbed the corporate ladder, and because of his hard work, commitment and determination over many years he was rewarded with significant financial success. He had financial security and did not want for anything, and could spend the rest of his days living very comfortably. However, to attain this financial security, he had spent immense amounts of times away from his family – it was not handed to him on a platter. My friend had a father who was frequently absent from her life due to his work commitments. My friend's auntie, on the other hand, lived a comfortable lifestyle with less significant assets. It is likely that my friend's grandmother, in her innocence, concluded that her son did not need her assets while giving them to her daughter would provide her with much more comfort and financial security.

I asked my friend's father how he felt being left out of his mother's Will, and whether he felt angry. He replied that he was not angry, he was just devastated, totally devastated, and felt that he did not mean anything to his mother, that she did not love him. This is a man in his seventies who is left to carry that hurt for the rest of his life because of the legacy his mother left behind.

On reflection, she most likely did love him very much. She did however make some grave mistakes in her Will. She should have clearly stipulated in her Will why she had not made any provision for her son, so that he was validated and he had answers as to why he did not receive an inheritance from his mother.

Secondly, she perhaps should have had an open and frank conversation with him as to what the contents of her Will were, particularly when she had previously on occasion advised that everything was to be split equally between her two children.

When my clients advise me that they wish to omit someone from their Will who may by the outside world be deemed to be a natural beneficiary of a Will, I encourage my clients to clearly address this issue in the Will. We insert a provision in their Will acknowledging that a particular person has been left out of the Will and stipulate the reason why that person has been left out. It may or may not provide comfort to the person who has been left out of the Will when and if they read it.

As well as providing an explanation as to why that person has been omitted from the Will we are also providing some guidance to any prospective Court as to what my client's intentions were and why they put this provision in place, which can play a pivotal role in the event that a claim is brought against the estate by the person who has been omitted from the Will.

In addition, if you think that the person you wish to omit from your Will is likely to bring a claim against your estate as a result of being omitted, you may give consideration to leaving them a nominal sum in your Will which may mitigate any claim being brought against your estate.

It is also important to remember that just because a person brings a claim against your estate when you are no longer here does not mean that their claim will be successful. There are a number of factors that the Courts consider in respect to such applications, however the strategies suggested within this chapter may go some way to assist the Courts in determining their decision on the matter before them, particularly in understanding what your intentions were at the time of putting your Will in place.

A client I acted for had four children, two sons and two daughters. He was estranged from all children aside from one daughter. He had not had a meaningful relationship with some of his children for over fifteen years, and being in his later years he did not see any prospect of reconciling with them. He still wished to acknowledge all his children in his Will and left various proportions of his estate to them. He conceded to me during one of our chats that he had given serious consideration to making no provision in his Will for two of his children, but did not think that was the moral thing to do; he still felt he had a moral duty to make provisions for all his children, regardless that it was for varying amounts.

If you are considering not leaving money to a child because they have a dependency issue or cannot control their own money I encourage you to read chapter eighteen of this book, which deals with making provision for children who cannot control their own inheritance. It will give you some options and food for thought that will help you make an informed decision regarding your inheritance for your child.

BLENDED FAMILIES

Blended relationships are very common these days. There appears to be a trend towards each party in the relationship to want their assets to end up with their own children from a previous relationship, especially where both parties are financially secure. In such cases, it is commonplace to stipulate that you have not made any provision for your spouse or partner, whichever the case may be, in your Will as you both desire that your own individual wealth ends up with your own children and that your partner or spouse has their own financial means.

Your assets are yours to do and leave as you wish. If you do determine not to make provision for a child or other beneficiary who would normally be assumed to be a beneficiary in your Will, the key takeaway should be that it is really helpful to document your reasons why no provision is being made for that person as it provides guidance for the people you leave behind, rather than leaving unanswered questions as to why they were left out of your Will. For some the reasons may be glaringly obvious, for others this may not be so.

Live the way you want
to be remembered.

Author Unknown

Chapter twenty-one

Let's not forget the fur babies

Pets have become an integral part of families; there has been many a time that clients have confessed that they sometimes like their pets more than their children. One only needs to look at the money spent on pets and the variety of items available to purchase for pets to know they are adored family members.

As a result, many clients are seeking to make provision for their pets in their Will. This may be by way of providing definitive direction in respect to who you would like to look after your pet if you are no longer here.

Obviously if you were a husband and wife and empty nesters then it would seem that the survivor would care for your pet. However, at the time that you are both not here, decisions would need to be made as to who would care for your much-loved pet. If you have someone in mind to care for your pets when you are no longer here it is a good idea to ask them if they would be agreeable to doing so.

PROVIDING FOR FUTURE CARE

Clients often leave a bequeath in their Will to the person who they wish to care for their pet. This provision is made along the lines of being used for their care and welfare and for future vet and grooming expenses.

In respect to the amount of this bequeath it can be a figure that aligns with you. Often this figure is aligned to the age of the pet and their life expectancy and whether your pet has any special requirements. I have a client who left an amount of ten thousand dollars to the person who was designated to care for her cat, for her cat's future care and other associated expenses. Another client left a similar amount for the care of her horses.

Legend has it that real estate mogul Leona Helmsley left her pet dog Trouble the mammoth sum of twelve million dollars at the time of her death in 2007. I am sure that most would agree that is an awful lot of indulgence on pet care and grooming.

Alternatively, you may not know anyone who would be willing to care for your pet but may have a preference in respect to a person or organisation who you would want your executor to engage with in finding a new home for your pet. It is therefore a good idea to list such wishes in your Will as they will provide guidance to your executor in respect to this matter.

Fur babies provide us with unconditional love while we are alive, so it is nice to return the gesture by caring for what happens to them when you are no longer here. Include them in your Estate Plan – they will be very happy that you do, even if they cannot tell you.

Make a difference.

Justice Michael Kirby

Chapter twenty-two

Technology, passwords and social media

When putting an Estate Plan in place, it is also important to consider what sort of digital legacy you would like to leave behind. It is an ideal time to consider your passwords, social media and email accounts, and what will happen to these when you die.

What about your social media accounts? They keep you connected with so many others during your lifetime, but have you given any thought to what you would like to happen to these social media accounts when you die? The reality is that these accounts are most likely going to outlive you, and different social media platforms have different criteria in respect to your accounts when you are no longer here.

Facebook alone has more than one billion active monthly users, and it is likely that in the next few years the estimated number of dead Facebook account holders will outnumber living Facebook users. A very interesting thought to ponder.

MEMORIALISING ACCOUNTS

Some people spend years building up their social media profiles and they may contain special photos and memories, so you may want these to be retained for your family, loved ones or friends.

If you have Facebook and Instagram accounts, what would you

like to happen to them? Both Facebook and Instagram allow for your profile to be memorialised when you are no longer here.

If you wish for your Facebook profile to be memorialised your executor would seek to become a legacy contact and would be able to take control of some aspect of your account after your death. Your executor would be able to place a final message on your Facebook profile prior to it being turned into a memorialised profile. Your Facebook friends would then be able to continue to post on your Facebook profile page should they wish to.

In respect to memorialised Instagram accounts your profile may not be changed by your executor or loved one and no one can log into your profile.

Alternatively, you may wish for your Facebook and Instagram profiles to be deleted, and your executor may do this in accordance with your wishes after your death.

DELETING ACCOUNTS

Twitter and LinkedIn accounts may not be memorialised, however they do allow for these accounts to be deleted should you so wish.

Social media profiles is an evolving area of the law as the social media platforms usually enter into an agreement with you while you are alive in respect to their terms and conditions. Often, these user agreements add an element of complication as the companies that hold these platforms are in an overseas jurisdiction, distinct from our Australian jurisdiction.

To be as transparent as possible in respect to your social media platforms and your digital afterlife it's a good idea to leave clear instructions for your executor in your Will or Memorandum of Wishes in respect to what you would like to happen to your social media profiles and accounts subsequent to your death.

The same also applies to your email accounts. Your email accounts may contain important information that could be of assistance to your executor or other parties after your death. Do you wish your executor to access these email accounts, or would you prefer another trusted person had access to these accounts? Document these wishes so that everyone is clear in respect to what you would like to happen.

If you wish for your executor to access your social media or email accounts it is vital that you keep a list of your accounts and passwords in a secure place, and ensure that these are updated in the event that you set up a new account or change a password.

Below is a listing of the most popular social media accounts and the links to memorialise or delete an account or profile.

To memorialise an account

Facebook: https://www.facebook.com/help/contact/234739086860192
Instagram: https://help.instagram.com/contact/452224988254813?helpref=faq_content

To delete an account

Facebook: https://www.facebook.com/help/contact/228813257197480
Instagram: https://help.instagram.com/contact/1474899482730688?helpref=faq_content
Linkedin:https://www.linkedin.com/help/linkedin/answer/2842?query=deceased%20account
Twitter: https://help.twitter.com/forms/privacy
You Tube/Google Plus:
https://support.google.com/accounts/troubleshooter/6357590?hl=en#ts=6357652

PASSWORDS

All passwords that you have are of particular importance to your executor as they hold the key to valuable information that your executor may need. It is therefore imperative that your passwords are located in a secure place that your executor will be able to access subsequent to your death. I have had on many occasions executors advise me that the deceased had left instructions that all their passwords were kept under lock and key in a safe. Which is all well and good – except no one knew what the password was to open the safe and retrieve these passwords.

Passwords are sensitive information that should not be left lying around but kept in a safe place that a trusted source knows about or kept in a password manager program for which the trusted source knows the password. Some people elect to put in place a Digital Asset Register which lists all their digital assets, which is a comprehensive document that is particularly useful to your executor after your death.

Our world is consistently evolving, and with the emergence of social media in our lives our digital afterlife needs to be given considerable thought when putting our Estate Plan in place. It forms part of the legacy which you wish to leave behind, so your decisions may have a significant impact on those left behind.

One day, you'll just be a
memory to some people.
Do your best to be
a good one.

Author Unknown

Chapter twenty-three

Your important wishes

Often, people have important wishes they would like to document for when they are no longer here. These are often documented by way of a Memorandum of Wishes or by leaving letters to executors, guardians and loved ones.

Recently, I had a long conversation with a client who had been delaying putting her Estate Plan in place, particularly as it was so difficult to imagine her young daughter – who is an only child – growing up without her. She was terrified of not being able to see her young daughter grow up, and it was important for her that her daughter knew where she came from and what her hopes and aspirations were for her daughter.

Throughout the chat I encouraged my client to take some time over the coming weeks to sit down and write a letter to her daughter which told the story of her donor and where she came from, together with her family history. Once complete, this letter is then stored with my client's Will and other personal documents, and would only be opened and given to her daughter if the need arises and my client passes away prior to having the chat about her daughter's story and history with her.

I then encouraged my client to write a letter to her daughter's appointed guardian. Again, this letter was sealed and kept with my client's Will just in case it is required one day. The contents of the letter details how my client would like her daughter to be raised, the schools she would like her to attend, the traditions she would like her to continue to embrace, and so on.

LEAVING DIRECTIONS AND WISHES

I am a strong advocate of parents leaving directions and wishes to the appointed guardians of any minor children. One must be mindful that these are not legally binding, they are merely wish provisions. However, experience shows that guardians do find these wishes to be highly persuasive and most guardians try their best to adhere to them if possible.

I have a client who met the love of his life on the idyllic party island Mykonos many moons ago. His now wife is an Australian, so he ended up following her back to her native country, where they are very happily settled and have now created their own little family with four children. It was of paramount importance to my client that his children have a relationship with his family, who reside in France. Each year my client and his family return to France for the European summer to reconnect with his family.

In the event that something should befall my client and his wife it is his sincere wish that his children are to return to France every summer to continue this tradition and spend time with his blood family, the family he grew up with and has created so many memories with. We were able to document these wishes in his Estate Plan, and encouraged our client to expand on such wishes further in his letter of wishes to his children's guardian.

Some considerations that you may like to discuss in your letter to your children's guardian are:

- Do you wish your children to see family members/your close friends/Godparents periodically? For example, once a month, four times a year. Alternatively, you may wish for the children to see grandparents and other family members on special occasions, such as birthdays or Christmas.

- On your children's birthdays, are there certain traditions that you would like to be followed?
- On the anniversary of your birthday, are there certain traditions that you would like to be followed?
- At Christmas, are there certain traditions that you would like to be followed?
- Would you like your children to have a part-time job, and if so, at what age should they be encouraged to obtain such a job?
- In respect to your children's education, are there particular schools that you would like your children to attend?
- Would you like your children to undertake after-school activities, and if so, are there particular activities that you would like them to do?
- How often would you like your children to be taken on holidays? Would you like other family members or friends to have the opportunity to take your children on holidays?
- Are there any religious traditions that you would like your children to adhere to?
- Are there any customs that you would like your children to follow?

The above list is in no way exhaustive; it is merely a guide for you to think about what is important to you, and to write your letter to your children's guardian expressing your wishes for how you would like your children raised.

FINANCIAL INSTRUCTIONS

From a financial perspective I find that clients are conscious of ensuring that their children will be looked after, particularly if they are minors or young adults. They want to ensure that their children's inheritance is invested in the correct vehicles and that their children are provided for financially.

Likewise, it's also a good idea to leave a letter to your executor if you have specific wishes in respect to the financial aspects of your estate. By way of example, if you have specific advisors you would like your executor to engage and seek the advice of in respect to your assets, that should be included in your Will and may also be included in your letter to your executor, particularly if you wish to indicate the investments that you would like the executor to consider for your beneficiaries.

You may also like your children to receive funds to acquire a motor vehicle upon attaining their driver licence, and you may like to leave a direction to your executor in respect to this. Or, you may wish to provide funds for your children to have a gap year if they so wish, between finishing their secondary schooling and commencing tertiary studies, and accordingly you may wish to direct that your executor release an allocated sum for each of your children to do this.

There are no real limitations to what your wishes are, however I can only impress that if you do have directions and wishes that you would like to leave to your executor in respect to such matters that you must adequately document them so the executor has clarity in respect to what you would like to happen.

Earlier in this chapter I touched on a client leaving a letter to her young daughter. If you have young children, you can find a quiet space one day when the time is right and write a letter to them which expands on whatever is important that you want them to know. This could be their history, where they came from, significant moments in their early life that they may not remember, special times that you have shared together thus far, your hopes and wishes for their future together, with any advice that you would like to impart to them for their future. This task can be hard; it can feel peculiar writing your wishes regarding your children as you have an expectation that you will be here for a long time to come and it can in a sense seem like an irrelevant and pointless exercise.

But the reality is, we do not know how long we are here for. If you are fortunate enough to live for a long time and your letter is redundant, fantastic, you can rip it up once your children are adults and be thankful that it had no relevance. However, if you passed away unexpectedly and your children received your letter that by the time they read it may have been written some years ago, they will be extremely grateful that you cared enough about them to take the time to write them such a letter. The letter from you is a finality, something for them to hold on to and treasure forever.

Often a parent who knows they only have a short period of time left to live as a result of illness and who is fully aware of their own mortality will spend extensive amounts of time writing letters to their children, including birthday cards and notes for each upcoming birthday, Christmas and other special occasions. These are left behind to be given to their children on each relevant future occasion, and can add to the sense of connection that you are still here in some way when you are no longer here. It can be a lovely legacy for children left behind.

Letters of wishes are not just left behind for children, they can also be left behind for partners or spouses. Often at such emotional times in one's life when one's partner or spouse is dying, conversations that they would like to have are not had, often because they are deemed too emotional or difficult. Often because you each want to cherish all the time you have left, leaving a letter for a partner to read upon your death can provide the surviving partner with great comfort. This letter may include wishes about how you would like your partner to raise your children and can include encouragement that they can do it, that they are up to raising your children even though you are no longer here.

It is also an opportunity to give your blessing that they have your permission to re-partner when you are no longer here and the time is right, should that be your wish. Such gestures can be extremely meaningful and comforting to the partner left behind. Although it would be wonderful for couples to have these conversations in person while still alive, on occasions where it is too hard to have those difficult conversations, letters left behind can be both consoling and reassuring.

People who have been blessed to live to a wonderful ripe old age often also like to leave letters behind to family or friends. It may be to tell them a little about the family history or their life and how they would like to be remembered, or it may be to impart some final words of advice and guidance.

The lesson in all of this is, no matter what age you are, no matter if you are married, single, a parent or have no children, many of us have some little legacy, notes or wishes that we wish to leave behind. If this resonates with you and is important to you, find some time one day to sit down in a nice comfortable spot and write those letters, write those notes, document those wishes and then keep them all in a safe place together with your Will so that when the day comes they can be given to the person they are written for so they can read your final wishes, advice or guidance and receive some comfort.

The need to leave a legacy is our spiritual need to have a sense of meaning, purpose, personal congruence, and contribution.

Stephen Covey

Chapter twenty-four

Write those lists

I'm personally a strong advocate for making things as easy as possible for those who are left behind after your death. Losing a loved one is difficult; dealing with the affairs and estate of a loved one who has just passed away compounds grief. So, if you can leave your affairs in as pristine order as possible your executors and loved ones will be immensely thankful.

IMPORTANT DOCUMENTS

One of the best ways to do this is to compile some lists. It sounds simple and it is, however unfortunately many people do not heed this advice. On these lists you should include information in respect to where your important documents are held. Amongst the important documents to be listed are:

- Your original Will
- Your Birth Certificate
- Original Certificates of Titles for properties that you own
- Business Succession Agreements and Deeds
- Discretionary Trust Deeds
- Copies of Binding Death Nominations
- Insurance Policies

- Shareholding Certificates
- Prepaid Funeral documentation
- Memorandum of Wishes or other instructions to your executor
- Guardian Wishes
- Details of locations of safety deposit boxes held with a financial institution.

Identifying where these original documents are held will save your executor an enormous amount of time and stress. Many people frantically go searching for their Certificate of Title to no avail. It is important to note that if you have a mortgage over your property then the bank that provided this mortgage to you will hold your original Certificate of Title for that property until such time that the debt owed pertaining to that property is fully discharged.

THE KING OF LISTS

Some years ago, I had a lovely client attend my office to put his Estate Plan in place. As well as being a delightful person, he is one of the most efficient and organised people I have ever met. He came to me with a handful of lists. I will forever remember him as the King of Lists.

The first list contained all the details of his immediate family extending back to his parents, so that it also included his siblings and his wife's siblings together with details of their sibling's children, being his nieces and nephews. The list was effectively a family tree. It was so precise and clear as to where everyone fitted into the family and clearly defined what asset each family member was to receive. Now, this process is a little outside the box and I do not normally receive copies of client's family trees, but I must concede it made my job easier when putting in place his Estate Plan, and I am sure it would help an executor who was not familiar with the deceased's extended family dynamics immensely.

The next list contained every substantial asset that the client owned, inclusive of full bank account details and account numbers, all shareholdings and their relevant security numbers, property details for each property, clearly identifiable details for each motor vehicle, a full listing of current liabilities together with information in respect to full contact details of his accountant, financial advisor, stockbroker, mortgage broker and personal banker. Talk about attention to detail.

There was also a list which included the full name, email address, telephone number and postal address of each person that the client wanted the executor to contact to advise them of his demise. Some may say this is over the top, and perhaps it is. It does however make that executor's job so much easier in having a list to work through for following the deceased's wishes.

On another occasion I had an elderly client attend my office carrying a large folder labelled 'Things for when I am Dead'. Confronting, yes, but smart too, as his son – who is the executor of his Will – shall not have to go looking too far to find the relevant information he requires when his father is no longer here.

As I write this book, I am acting for executors who recently lost their brother to a terminal illness. Although he had been unwell for some time their brother did not believe the end was near, despite his declining health, and he therefore had not conveyed his important passwords to his executors. Despite their best attempts they have not been able to access his computer and other relevant accounts, as the passwords that they thought their brother would perhaps use have not proved successful in accessing the required information or accounts. There is a very good likelihood they will not be able to access some of the accounts they require, or if they do find a way to access them it is likely to take considerable time and cost, which could have been alleviated by their brother providing these passwords to them.

The executors conceded to me that in their brother's final days they did not think to ask him for the passwords. That is the reality; when someone is on their deathbed and you are watching them die you do not entertain thoughts about passwords. It is not the appropriate time; you want to cherish the final moments with a loved one. This serves as a reminder as to why everything needs to be put in place when you are able and capable, not when it is too late.

Of course, the whole point of having lists is redundant if you do not leave them in a safe place where the executor can find them upon your death. In talking of a safe place, I do not mean inside a safe deposit box or safe, unless you have given your executor or a family member the code to the safe deposit box or safe. Many a time I have had an executor come to me who has been unable to locate important documentation or obtain access to the deceased's safe.

I am an advocate of encouraging clients to sit down with their executor and letting them know where they will be able to locate all the important information that they will require upon their death. I am sure your executor will appreciate the chat, and appreciate the time and effort you have gone to in putting your affairs in place.

The best legacy you could leave is not some building that is named after you or a piece of jewellery but rather a world that has been impacted and touched by your presence, your joy, and your positive actions.

Jon Gordon

Chapter twenty-five

The final farewell

Well this is it. The Ending. Planning for the end of your life. Some people find this too confronting, or perhaps too morbid, others just do not want to think about it. To some it is a unique opportunity to organise their final farewell, their final legacy in their own way.

During my life I have lost loved ones, I have assisted clients with terminal illnesses and those towards the end of their lives with putting their final wishes in place and I have assisted grieving families. I understand the importance of the final farewell.

FUNERALS

Some of my clients have no desire for a funeral ceremony, a celebration of life or any formal acknowledgement of their passing, and if this is your wish it's important that you stipulate this in your Will so that your executor is aware.

Likewise, if you do have specific wishes relating to your final farewell, be sure to list them in your Will or leave detailed instructions in your personal papers with a copy of your Will so your executor knows what your wishes are. The more specific you are with your wishes the better. For instance, if it is your wish to be cremated and your ashes scattered at your favourite holiday location, document this wish so that people know. If you want no fanfare and to be cremated privately and your ashes scattered remotely, stipulate this. By providing clarity to those left behind you are alleviating them of what could be emotionally painful decision making.

DISPOSAL OF YOUR BODY

While we are on the topic of disposal of your body, I have heard all the jokes – I think it makes clients feel more comfortable when they discuss this topic with me. They feel uneasy discussing this topic, so they joke about it, and that is okay if it helps them come to a decision. I will say if I had a dollar for every client who has said to me, 'I want to be buried but what if I am still alive when they put me in a coffin and I can't get out', I would be a very rich woman. It happens in Hollywood movies, we have all heard stories of this happening in real life, and I haven't checked out how credible they are, however I think it is safe to say the medical professionals and funeral directors will follow due diligence and check that you have definitely passed away before placing you in your final resting place.

In recent times, I have found an emerging trend towards people having a celebration of life and ethical burials, and when I say celebration of life, I mean a *celebration* of life. An event where people are joyous as they remember and share the wonderful memories of time spent with you.

I personally find an element of beauty in those who plan their final farewell, whether it is leaving behind a note or even a poem to be read at their final farewell or whether it is to leave behind instructions to friends and family for how they would like the day to unfold, so in essence, a script of some sort. This is your last chance to command the centre stage, to leave your loved ones and all those who attend with a message, your message, a lasting legacy, something for them to hold on to and remember you by.

One of my clients owned a tea shop, and it was her simple wish that her farewell was to be held in the backyard of her family home with her favourite music playing and her favourite food and teas served. A personal anecdote to all that she was.

Decades ago Sandra West, a Beverley Hills socialite, determined in her Will that she should be buried inside her Ferrari with the seat 'slanted comfortably'. This request was certainly outside the box, however at least she left very clear instructions to her executor.

Some people have strong religious beliefs and wish to clearly stipulate the religious rituals they would like to be included in their farewell. Some people come from families who have strong religious beliefs that they personally do not hold or share.

One of my clients comes from a Macedonian background, however he held a strong belief that he did not want his funeral to be held in a Greek or Macedonian Church. Further, he did not want his funeral to be religious in nature and wanted the service to be held in English, not Greek or Macedonian. My client was adamant about these wishes being included in his Will as he knew that his parents, who held strong religious beliefs, would want him to have a funeral service in a Greek or Macedonian church and he did not wish for his wife, who was also the executor of his Will, to be confronted with external pressure from his parents in the event that anything happened to him. His wishes were clearly documented in his Will for his executor to follow.

This same client had compiled the music list to be played at his funeral and had also expressed his wish for his ashes to be scatted at the Holy Grail of sport in Melbourne, the iconic MCG. I did explain that I was not so sure that the scattering of his ashes at this iconic venue was legally allowed. He did kindly respond where there is a will there is a way, and invariably he will be scattered by family members in a moment of naughtiness after an AFL game when patrons are allowed on the surface for a game of kick to kick.

A few years ago, I had the utmost privilege of acting for one of the most radiant ladies I have had the pleasure of knowing. She was gracious, elegant, engaging and so full of life, all this even though she had a terminal illness and time was slipping away from her quickly.

In putting her Estate Plan in place there was a strong emphasis on her final farewell, as there was no way this lady was going out with a whimper.

At her funeral, a few weeks later, her final wishes were carried out. Aside from the congregation being instructed to wear her favourite colour, she left her final act to the end. At the conclusion of her funeral service out came six very handsome male models, wearing sleek black pants and pink bow ties, but otherwise they were topless and caused much commotion amongst the congregation when they first appeared. They accompanied her coffin down the aisle to much laughter from the congregation. My client had got her wish: she did not want a sad, tearful ending, she wanted laughter and joy, and by all accounts she certainly got that. Her single final act will be remembered by many and I am sure will continue to put a smile on their faces every time they think of this memory.

Sometimes people do not realise the legacy they will leave behind. My gorgeous father died suddenly and unexpectedly. His funeral was attended by hundreds, so much so that the chapel was overflowing, and my most profound memory was leaving the chapel behind my father's casket with my mother and siblings to see a guard of honour formed by his former colleagues from the Metropolitan Fire Brigade, an organisation that he had retired from over fifteen years prior. It was unexpected and appreciated, and my dad would have absolutely loved it, together with the two fire trucks that were also in attendance that day. I remember some of my closest friends saying that it was evident the impact that my father had on people when they saw his colleagues, grown up men, with tears in their eyes as his casket passed by them.

So, I implore you to remember this: you may not realise the legacy you are leaving behind or the impact that you have on people. I do however hope that this book encourages you to plan your final farewell, no matter how little or big you would like it to be. Do it your way.

It's the little moments
that make life big.

Kobi Yamada

Chapter twenty-six

Still here, but incapacitated

Many people only think it is relevant to put a Will in place and then your Estate Plan is all ticked off. However, what would happen if you are in a serious car accident and end up in the intensive care unit of your local hospital? You sustain brain injuries, and your body is wrecked, you spend a month in intensive care and then go to a rehabilitation facility for an extended period. Or alternatively, you are out one night for dinner with friends having a joyous time and in the next instant you have a stroke, with the devastating effect that you are now totally incapacitated and can no longer make decisions for yourself.

Who will run your business? Who will look after your investments and other financial interests, inclusive of paying your daily household bills? Who will care for you and decide where you will live?

Most people do not like to think of these incidents happening as they are way too daunting and far removed from our daily lives – unless of course you know someone who has suffered a deliberating change of capacity so quickly. We think we are all immune to this, that it happens to others, but the reality is that it can happen to us too, normal people like you and me.

So, it's crucial that you consider this eventuality as part of your Estate Plan and put the relevant documents in place so that the people that you want to make decisions on your behalf in respect to financial, legal, guardianship and medical decisions if you can no longer make decisions for yourself will be the people making such decisions for you.

If you don't put these documents in place you are leaving everything to chance, and it may mean someone you would not want to make decisions for you may in fact be granted authority to make decisions on your behalf in the event that you become incapacitated.

DON'T WAIT

Many people think that you only need to make provisions for these documents when you get old. When you get old, you most certainly should put these documents in place, particularly as dementia and Alzheimer's are becoming more prevalent in our society with many people living longer. However, it is important to remember dementia and Alzheimer's are not just 'old people' diseases.

Some years ago, I acted for a client, let us call her Monique. Monique had extensive business and investment interests, she was an Appointor of several Discretionary Trusts, a director and secretary of various entities, as well as being unit holder of a number of Unit Trusts, and she had various other business interests. She was also a dedicated and loving mother to seven children; the youngest children attended primary school with the remaining children attending secondary schooling.

Two years after putting her extensive Estate Plan in place we were contacted by Monique's husband and advised that Monique had dementia at just 46 years of age. Sadly, Monique's health deteriorated rapidly, and it was not long before she could no longer remember her young children's names and could not partake as a fully operational member of her family. A carer was hired to look after her in a full-time capacity, and the family also acquired a nanny to look after and care for the younger children as well as assist with transportation to school, sport and other after-school and weekend activities, activities that Monique had attentively attended to prior to dementia diminishing her health. Monique's family were fortunate that they had the funds to afford such assistance to help with Monique's and her family's everyday needs, particularly in light of the fact that her husband now had the sole responsibility of looking after the family's various business interests.

Crucially, as Monique had taken the time to put in place a well-considered estate plan, her Power of Attorney could be used extensively for both her business interests and personal interests, so her family and business interests were not impacted significantly as her appointed attorney could act under the provisions of her Power of Attorney document.

If Monique had not put a Power of Attorney in place it would have been a totally different story – it would have had the capacity to impact her business interests in the short term, potentially led to family conflict and no doubt enormous stress. This was a small positive out of a shocking diagnosis. Monique's young family and her husband suffered as her health continued to deteriorate; she was no longer the person they knew, and devastatingly at the age of fifty-two she passed away. I gently repeat, dementia is not an old people's disease. Monique's story shows it can happen at any age.

Around the same time that Monique was diagnosed a friend contacted me in relation to one of her colleagues. She and her husband, Tom had separated just over eighteen months prior, they shared custody of their two young children and were in the process of finalising their divorce and property settlement with the court.

Then disaster struck: at the age of forty-two Tom had a massive stroke which rendered him permanently incapacitated. He could not communicate, he could not walk and he had limited movement. He needed full-time care for the rest of his life.

Tom had no Estate Plan in place, hence had not made provisions for a Power of Attorney. He was recently separated with two young children and a relatively fractured maternal family. To put it plainly, Tom was in a horrific situation. Given the unexpected demise of Tom's health and the emotions involved, cracks started to show amongst his siblings and parents. They were in conflict in respect to who would be the best person to care for Tom and his financial and legal interests going forward.

In Victoria, where Tom resides, if someone can no longer make decisions for themselves and do not have Power of Attorney documents in place, application needs to be made to the Victorian Civil and Administrative Tribunal (VCAT) for a Guardian and Administrator to be appointed to make decisions on their behalf. In Tom's case three interested parties made an application to VCAT to be appointed both Tom's Guardian and Appointor.

Based on the applications made and based on Tom's medical records and other relevant information submitted to VCAT, a determination was made in respect to who was appointed Tom's Guardian and Appointor. The VCAT representative making this decision is a person who did not know Tom nor did they have any idea of who Tom would want to care for his needs. If you were in Tom's situation, would you wish for such a decision to be made by a person you have never even met? The VCAT application made on Tom's behalf – which created conflict and stress and took considerable time – could have been avoided if Tom had put in place the relevant Power of Attorney documents while he had the capacity to do so.

Tom's story is devastating. His wife and children were also severely impacted as court proceedings had not been finalised and his wife was consequently left financially disadvantaged to bring up their two young children alone.

THE DIFFERENT TYPES OF POWER OF ATTORNEY DOCUMENTS

There are a number of different types of Power of Attorney documents that you may put in place, dependent on which state or territory you reside in and where your assets are held. A listing of the prescribed documents for each state is provided later in this chapter. The most common Power of Attorney documents are:

- A **Specific Power of Attorney** is usually put in place for a specific purpose, for instance you intended to sell a property and wished for someone to act on your behalf in respect to the sale of the property. Once that purpose has been satisfied the Specific Power of Attorney is redundant.
- An **Enduring Power of Attorney** is the most common Power of Attorney that people put in place. In some states and territories, it relates solely to appointing someone to make financial and legal decisions on your behalf, while in other states this document allows your attorney to make financial, legal, medical and personal decisions on your behalf.
- **Enduring Guardianship** is a document that allows you to appoint someone to make medical and personal decisions on your behalf.
- An **Appointment of Medical Treatment Decision Maker** allows you to appoint someone to make medical and lifestyle decisions on your behalf.

WHO SHOULD YOU APPOINT AS YOUR ATTORNEY?

Choosing who to appoint as your attorney is a very personal decision. It really comes down to who you trust to make the best decisions for you in accordance with your wishes.

In most cases a married couple will have each other as their attorney in the first instance. If their spouse is unable to undertake the role of attorney for whatever reason then they may appoint one of their adult children, a sibling, a parent, or a close friend.

It is common for people to appoint different people for each document. By way of example, you may have a child who is extremely savvy from a financial perspective, understands investments and legalities surrounding finances and property who you may wish to appoint as your attorney in respect to your Enduring Power of Attorney. This child may also be emotionally disconnected to all medical matters and so you may be inclined to appoint someone else to be your medical treatment decision maker in respect to your Appointment of Medical Treatment Decision Maker.

In a number of the Power of Attorney documents you may also appoint more than one attorney, should you wish. They may also act jointly or jointly and severally, and it is important that you stipulate the manner in which you would like them to act on your prescribed Power of Attorney documents.

WHEN DOES A POWER OF ATTORNEY COME INTO EFFECT?

The actual date that a Power of Attorney commences can vary between different states and the information contained in some of the prescribed Power of Attorney forms. Generally, a Power of Attorney can come into effect immediately upon signing your Power of Attorney or it can come into effect when you are deemed to no longer have capacity to make your own decisions. In most cases, the Power of Attorney forms allow you to stipulate when you would like these powers to commence.

There are comparable arguments for and against your Power of Attorney commencing immediately upon signing your Power of Attorney document. If you are someone who travels extensively as well as operates your own business, you may wish for your spouse to have the authority to sign important documents while you are away.

Alternatively, we have several elderly clients who have limited mobility and do not have internet banking or are not comfortable using technology. Such clients often rely on their children or another trusted person to attend to the payment of household bills or their banking so having a Power of Attorney in place assists their attorney in attending to these tasks. This also allows their attorney to communicate with government agencies such as Centrelink or utility and service companies on their behalf should the person putting the Power of Attorney document in place wish for them to do so.

Alternatively, you may deem that it is not necessary for your Power of Attorney to come into effect immediately and you may wish for it to commence only in the event that you become incapacitated and can no longer make decisions for yourself.

HOW LONG DOES A POWER OF ATTORNEY LAST?

In all jurisdictions of Australia, a Power of Attorney ceases at the time of your death or if you revoke your Power of Attorney. You may revoke a Power of Attorney at any time by completing the prescribed revocation form. Alternatively, if you put in place a new Power of Attorney this will automatically revoke any previous Power of Attorney documents that you may have in place.

Each jurisdiction in Australia currently has different prescribed Power of Attorney documents. In some states all requirements are combined into one single form, while in other states there are a number of different forms that are required to capture all relevant information. Below is a table of each state's and territories' requirements.

Victoria	• **Enduring Power of Attorney** for financial, legal and guardianship decisions • **Appointment of Medical Treatment Decision Maker** for medical treatment decisions • **Advance Care Directive** – medical wishes
New South Wales	• **Enduring Power of Attorney** for financial and legal decisions • **Enduring Guardianship** for lifestyle, health & medical decisions

Queensland	• **Enduring Power of Attorney** for financial and personal decisions • **General Power of Attorney** for financial decisions only
South Australia	• **Enduring Power of Attorney** for financial and legal decisions • **Advance Care Directive** wishes, preferences and instructions for your future health care, end of life, living arrangements and personal matters
Western Australia	• **Enduring Power of Attorney** for property and financial decisions • **Enduring Power of Guardianship** for personal, lifestyle and medical decisions. • **Advance Health Directive** (Similar to Advance Care Directive; see above)
Australian Capital Territory	• **Enduring Power of Attorney** financial, healthcare, personal and medical decisions
Northern Territory	• **Power of Attorney** for property matters • **Advance Personal Plan** for health, financial and life choices
Tasmania	• **Enduring Power of Attorney** for financial and property decisions • **Enduring Guardianship** for personal and medical decisions

In addition, some states require you to register Power of Attorney documents, particularly for land and property transactions. The following shows the registration requirements for each state.

Victoria	You do not need to register your documents.
New South Wales	You must Register your Power of Attorney if your attorney is going to sell, mortgage, lease or otherwise deal with your real estate. Otherwise it is not necessary to register it. However, by registering your Power of Attorney it will be on record as a public document, safe from loss or destruction, more easily accepted as evidence that your attorney is allowed to deal with your legal and financial affairs. Power of Attorneys are registered at the Sydney Office of Land and Property Information. Level 30/175 Liverpool St, Sydney NSW 2000
Queensland	The Power of Attorney or Enduring Power of Attorney must be registered at the Titles Registry if your attorney is going to act in respect of any land dealings. Titles Registry Office Level 11, 53 Albert Street (cnr Margaret Street), Brisbane City QLD 4000
South Australia	Enduring Power of Attorney needs to be registered at Land Titles office if it deals with property. Land Titles Office 101 Grenfell St, Adelaide SA 5000

Western Australia	There is no need to register a Power of Attorney in Western Australia. However, if the donor owns land or property, they may want to consider leaving their Power of Attorney with Landgate. Landgate 1 Midland Square, Midland WA 6056
Australian Capital Territory	Enduring Power of Attorney does not need to be registered unless being used in respect of dealing with land. If Power of Attorney is being used for this purpose, the original document must be registered at the Australian Capital Territory Office of Regulatory Service and a small fee is payable. Access Canberra Service Centre Swanson Plaza, Swanson Ct, Belconnen ACT 2617
Northern Territory	Register your Power of Attorney at the Land Titles Office for property or land. Land Titles Office Darwin Nichols Place, Corner Cavenagh and Bennett Streets Alice Springs Centrepoint Building, Corner Gregory Terrace and Hartley Streets

Tasmania	Enduring Power of Attorney – lodge with Land Titles Office. Approximately $147 Enduring Power of Attorney has no legal effect unless it is registered with the Recorder of Titles at the Land Titles Office. Enduring Guardianship – register with the Guardianship and Administration Board Land Titles Office 1/134 Macquarie St, Hobart TAS 7000

Having your Power of Attorney documents in place will empower you to make decisions for your future in the knowledge that your rights will be protected.

WHAT HAPPENS IF YOU DO NOT HAVE A POWER OF ATTORNEY IN PLACE AND YOU BECOME INCAPACITATED?

This is a very important question and one that I wish people knew the answer to so that they clearly understood the importance of putting these documents in place. Put simply, if you don't have them in place and you can no longer make your own decisions, you, or more to the point, your family or loved ones are in a little bit of a pickle.

Each state has their own relevant body or tribunal where someone, normally a family member or close friend, would have to make application to be appointed to make decisions on your behalf in respect to your financial, legal, medical and guardianship needs.

Some years ago, I acted for two adult sons. Their father, who we shall call Bill, had suffered several falls at home. His much younger second wife determined she no longer wished to care for Bill and returned overseas to her home country to reside. Bill was taken to hospital because of his injuries and tests were conducted to ascertain the cause of these frequent falls, together with other cognitive issues that were of concern. Upon receiving the results of the tests, it was determined by medical specialists that Bill no longer had the capacity to care for himself and make his own decisions. Given that Bill no longer had the capacity to put in place Power of Attorney documents, and given that Bill was a Victorian resident, his sons had to make an application to the Victorian Civil and Administrative Tribunal ('VCAT') to have them appointed as Bill's Administrator and Guardian.

The medical advice stipulated that Bill could no longer care for himself in his own home and with no family member being in a position to have Bill reside with them due to extensive work commitments, the sons commenced searching for a suitable nursing home in which to place Bill. A suitable nursing home, with a rare available opening for a new resident, was located, much to the family's relief. However, as with most nursing homes these days, one of the entry requirements was that a valid Enduring Power of Attorney was required upon acceptance to the nursing home. Bill did not have the converted document, so Bill was refused admission into the nursing home until such time that an Administrator and Guardian were appointed by VCAT.

Given the time to prepare the appropriate document and obtain the appropriate reports from medical staff and social workers that VCAT required to be submitted with the son's application, together with a backlog with the Tribunal's hearing listing, it was a number of weeks before the sons were able to obtain a VCAT order appointing them as their father's Administrator and Guardian. Bill remained in his local hospital for the duration of this time; after the VCAT order he was finally able to be moved to his chosen nursing home. As you can see, this is a process and can cause undue stress on family members and loved ones. Fortunately, in Bill's case he had family members looking after his best interests who were able to make solid decisions in respect to his care, financial and legal matters. Not all people have that luxury, especially when it is ultimately in the hands of the tribunal in determining who is the best person to look after your interests.

There have been countless times over my career as an estate planning lawyer where I have not been able to assist clients, particularly older clients, with putting in place their Power of Attorney documents simply because they no longer have the comprehension to understand documents due to their incapacity. It's devastating not being able to assist them in this regard. So many people leave it too late, which is one of the reasons I am an advocate for adult children having a chat with their parents to ensure that their parents have the appropriate Power of Attorney documents in place. By doing so they may be fortunate enough not to experience the same stress and predicament that Bill's family were confronted with.

I will touch on my previous point earlier in this chapter that it is not just older people who leave it too long to put Power of Attorney documents in place. Last year I was contacted by a lady, Hillary, who made some initial enquiries regarding putting Power of Attorney documents in place for her mother. I attended upon her mother and put her Power of Attorney documents in place for her.

Two days ago, I received a distressing telephone call from Hillary's partner who advised that Hillary was in hospital having suffered a terrible stroke a week ago. Did she have her Power of Attorney documents in place? No. There is something important conveyed in the analogy about fastening your own life jacket first before helping others. It is lovely that Hillary helped her mother, but she should have also taken care of her own Power of Attorney and Estate Plan before it became too late.

I often compare Power of Attorney documents to insurance. You put them in place, and you hope that you never need to use them – they are there just in case. The reality for most of us is that there are certain people we would like to care for us if we were no longer able to care for ourselves and make our own decision. Putting Power of Attorney documents in place goes a long way in providing peace of mind that we are covered if we are still here but can no longer make our own decisions.

At least once a day allow yourself the freedom to think and dream for yourself.

Albert Einstein

Chapter twenty-seven

Letting others know your medical wishes

Medical wishes. These are important wishes that again, a significant number of us do not consider until we are faced with our own mortality or have perhaps experienced the loss of a loved one. Many of us are guilty of thinking of life and death and forget about the bits in the middle or near the end.

I have innumerable conversations with people. I love to listen, and I love to hear people's stories. You learn so much by listening to stories. Everyone has a story. I also hear people's fears when telling their story. I hear the stories they tell about the dear old next-door neighbour who was in a terrible accident and that they heard from her son that she lingered on life support and she had told them over the fence last summer when they were chatting about the thriving vegetable garden she had created that was the last thing she would ever want to happen to her. If she was on life support, she wanted out. She had lived a good innings, she didn't want to linger on.

DISCUSSIONS WITH YOUR FAMILY

After telling me such stories clients then advise that it would be dreadful if the same thing happened to them as that is certainly not what they would wish to occur if they were in the same situation as their dear elderly neighbour had been. I then ask my client, have they expressed these wishes in writing to their family and I get their answer: NO.

Or alternatively they may answer I have told my family, but they do not want to talk about it. Interesting. Let me tell you, if they don't want to know about it, chances are your family switched off when you were speaking about it and collectively did not hear correctly what your wishes were. The spoken word is an interesting one, you can say the same thing to three people in the same context and they may all have different variations of what was actually said. One may have heard mum wants to be resuscitated, the other may have heard mum does not want to be resuscitated, and the third has no idea at all because they had totally zoned out.

Medical wishes are important; they are about your care, what you do and do not consent to, and include your crucial wishes if your time on earth is coming to an end. They matter. It is why it is imperative that you document this in writing, so that everyone is on the same page, your family, your loved ones, and the medical professionals.

ADVANCE CARE DIRECTIVES

The Advance Care Directive is a document that allows you to clearly document all your medical wishes and other relevant matters that are important to you. Having this document in place provides comprehensive guidance in respect to what you would like to happen in respect to your medical treatment and wishes, and helps to remove some of the emotion when such decisions need to be made.

Some of you may have extremely close families where everyone knows what your medical wishes are and what you would like to occur if you were near the end of your life, and that is fantastic, particularly if such important conversations have been had and written guidance has been provided. However, for many it may not be a conversation that they have with a loved one, or alternatively you may not have close loved ones and may have chosen a friend or associate to make these decisions on your behalf and they do not explicitly know what your wishes are.

The Advance Care Directive allows you to stipulate what is important to you, what matters most to you. For most people, this can revolve around being independent and continuing to reside in your own home, not being a burden to your family and being able to be cared for in your own home if possible.

It also allows you to stipulate what medical treatment you consent to and what medical treatment you do not consent to. Clients often ask me for guidance in respect to this and my answer is always the same: there is no right or wrong answer, it is what is important to you. The most common factors people stipulate revolve around their sentiments in respect to resuscitation, life support and treatment for cancer. I have had clients stipulate that should they develop brain cancer they do not wish to have any chemotherapy; I have had clients say that they want to be kept alive at all costs if they were on life support, others say if they are being kept alive by artificial means and have no brain function it is their wish that all life support is switched off. All these are very personal decisions that only you can make.

One of my clients, as well as being an extremely successful business owner with extensive business interests, is a mad Essendon Football Club supporter. He loves football more than life at times. His wish is that if he is near the end of his life he would like his room decorated in black and red, with an array of black and red balloons and the team song handy in case he would like to listen to it. To some it might be crazy, but to him it is what is important to him and how he would like to live out his final moments.

Others may have spiritual or religious beliefs that are important to them as they near the end of life. It is important that these are documented in your Advance Care Directive. If it is important that a priest visits you for the last rites, express this wish in your Advance Care Directive, so that your loved ones know this is important to you and can arrange for this to occur.

Some years ago, a family member spent her last day in hospital surrounded by her loving family, with the television on the Australian Open tennis which she loved and watched religiously each year, with her favourite radio station on in the background. For the later part she was unconscious, however I think she would have been happy with her ending, surrounded by those she loved with her favourite music and one of her favourite sports.

The Advance Care Directive essentially allows you the opportunity to include those things that are important to you if your life is coming to an end.

You may be thinking, I am so young I do not need to worry about these sorts of matters yet. Think again. I am fortunate to be part of an amazing group of lawyers across Australia, spearheaded by Clarissa Rayward of Happy Lawyer, Happy Life fame. Recently, one of the lawyers in our Club, a bright, vibrant lawyer who was doing amazing things in her life, making a wonderful difference to people's lives, was diagnosed with brain cancer. She was aged 39. She was a mother with three young children. Three weeks later she died. Just like that. Cancer does not discriminate; age does not discriminate. You may think you have a lot of time left, however sometimes that choice is taken out of your hands.

The Advance Care Directive is a document that I would really encourage you to put in place. Yes, it will be challenging and thought provoking, it may make you question your mortality, however on the flip side it empowers you to make decisions about your medical wishes and end-of-life wishes that hopefully will never have to be actioned, but one day they just might need to be. By having these wishes in place your family and loved ones will have a clear understanding of what you would like to happen, and they can also provide clear instructions to the medical profession in respect to what your wishes are. Essentially, by having the Advance Care Directive in place you can take comfort that your wishes are documented and that these will be followed should the time come.

At the end of life, what really matters is not what we bought, but what we built; not what we got, but what we shared; not our competence, but our character; and not our success, but our significance. Live a life that matters. Live a life of love.

Author Unknown

Chapter twenty-eight

Different ways to leave a legacy

Legacy means different things to so many different people. To some it may mean spending their life working hard to create something of significance to them to leave behind.

For others, their legacy is enshrined in having buildings, stadiums or monuments named after them. Sporting stars often have stands or stadiums named after them, eminent businesspeople or those involved in public life also frequently have rooms, halls, galleries and other significant venues named in their honour as a lasting legacy.

FINANCIAL LEGACIES

Some prominent entrepreneurs such as Richard Branson have built empires with airlines, gyms, record labels or hotels bearing their name. Clever self-promotion and marketing in one sense with an emphasis on their brand and the legacy that they want to leave behind.

Some wealthy benefactors have donated funds to a hospital on the provision that a wing in the hospital is named after them, so again their legacy lives on.

Others – like Australian billionaire Andrew Forrest and his wife Nicola – have pledged to give the majority of their wealth away during their lifetime, having established the Minderoo Foundation, a philanthropic organisation with two billion dollars currently committed to a range of global initiatives. Amongst the initiatives listed on the Minderoo Foundation's website are:

- creating employment parity for Indigenous Australians
- ensuring every child has a bright future
- collaboration against cancer
- returning oceans to a flourishing state
- building a digital ecology that empowers people.

These initiatives are diverse and have the ability to impact a formidable number of people as well as the environment, and materialise solely because the richest man in our country and his wife wanted to make a difference. What a beautiful legacy that is.

A LOCAL LEGACY

My own father lived in the same town his entire life; despite being well travelled there was no way he was ever going to live anywhere else. His family had lived there for generations, there was a road named after the family, and there is even a Sloan's Hill and a renowned cottage in the town named Sloan's cottage. Dad was heavily involved in the local football club; he was an extremely passionate supporter and I think I can say on authority that he was also one of their most vocal supporters. Upon his death, my family organised for a trophy to be awarded each year in his honour to a valued player – it is a way to continue his legacy in a place where he spent so much time and which was a significant part of his life. My father has been departed ten years now, but each year, one talented footballer receives the honour of a trophy in my father's name, and my father's memory is still embodied within that football club. His legacy lives on.

DOCUMENTING YOUR LIFE

A few years ago, I had a wonderful client who was nearing the end of his life at the age of 92. He liked to chat and was more than happy to engage you with stories about his life. That is what he held within him, stories. When he was gone, some of those stories would remain entrenched in the memories of family members, however with many friends now passed on there was not a large audience remaining to be custodians of those stories.

In the final eighteen months of his life he engaged a lady to visit him on a regular basis to sit and listen to him chat and transcribe his stories. My client's biography was finalised a couple of months prior to his death, a lovely legacy to leave behind for future generations of his family. As someone who never met one set of grandparents because they passed before I was born, I personally think it is a beautiful gift to leave behind. There are so many families who chat about relatives and wonder what certain situations or parts of their lives were like, the missing gaps. Leaving your story in written words may go some way to answering those missing gaps.

Others may prefer to do a video or audiobook of their story. This can also be a valuable gift to leave behind which can be viewed or listened to on occasion.

Within my own law firm, we offer clients a number of products that they can use in documenting their legacy. One such product is a beautifully presented document called My Story. It is a document with questions for them to answer about their life journey, from where they grew up, their favourite memories, relationships, and words of wisdom that they would like to leave behind.

Another document we offer is My Favourite Memories. This is a booklet that allows family members and friends to share their favourite memory of a loved one who has passed and is a lovely keepsake for their family. This is particularly so where they may have left behind young children who have limited memories of their parent who has now died.

There are also simple ways to leave a legacy. I have often heard of a particular plant being provided to mourners at a funeral or celebration of life so that the recipient may go home and plant this gift in their garden in memory of the person who has departed, a reminder of this person every time this plant blooms.

FAMILY TRADITIONS

Legacy is prevalent in many family traditions. I have fond recollections of my parents preparing the Christmas pudding and Christmas cake together each year with recipes handed down from my grandmother. Often such recipes can be handed down many generations, which leads to a lovely legacy. This is particularly so when families or friends come together for traditions and celebrations, and those that are no longer with us physically remain with us by way of the legacy they left behind.

Recently, I came across a wonderful beach property called Legacy and I could not stop thinking how wonderful this was. The parents who were the original owners of the property had left a beach property to their adult children, so that their adult children and their families could enjoy the long-held family tradition of spending time together at the beach shack enjoying each other's company and creating memories. With such an embodying intention I think this is one of the most appropriately named properties I have ever seen.

Legacy can also occur simply by your actions to inspire people. When you inspire people, a little part of you may stay with them. There is inspiration all around us and everyone can make a difference to the lives of others.

I love the iconic Maya Angelou quote: 'I've learned that people will forget what you said, people will forget what you did, but people will never forget how you made them feel.' I think it is a testament to the fact that people desire to feel wanted, special or loved, and when someone takes the time to make you feel special and that you matter, people remember that. A simple little act of making people feel special can create a legacy to last a lifetime.

REPUTATION

I recall many years ago I went to the MCG with my family to watch a one-day international cricket match in which Australia was playing the West Indies. We were fortunate to have seats in the inner alcoves of the MCC; as a cricket-mad young child growing up in a family with older brothers this is where you want to be because it is where your heroes walk the long path from the change rooms to the lush green surface of the most prized surface in Australia. The trick was to get there early and nab your hero as they walked that long path onto the oval to warm up prior to the commencement of the match. I had my eye on my favourite star, my autograph book in hand held out to him, willing him to sign my most prized possession at the time, when he rudely walked straight past ignoring all requests from fans for a few precious moments of his time.

As a young child I felt shattered, I cannot recall if I cried but I was mighty close if I didn't. In that moment, my perception of that well-known Australian cricketer was changed forever. Did I look at him the same way? No. Was a positive legacy left in my mind? No. Being a young mad sports fan, all was not lost; I quickly moved on to another favourite player, who for the record was happy to sign my little autograph book. I always remember how my new favourite player made me feel.

Throughout my life I have always drawn inspiration from people who I greatly admire and by whom I am inspired, and in their own little way they are leaving a legacy, perhaps not realising the impact they have had or the difference they have made to my life. I am not alone with this; I will impress that we all have the ability to make a difference and to be a shining light in people's lives. I was fortunate enough to meet Justice Kirby of the High Court of Australia some years ago. I purchased one of his books on the evening and he obliged in personally signing it and inscribing the words 'Make a Difference'. From that day forward those words have been permanently entrusted in all that I do and to this day inspire all that I do.

At the time of writing this book, the American jurist Ruth Bader Ginsburg had recently died. As an Associate Justice of the Supreme Court of the United States she was a woman of enormous influence, not only in America but around the world. She used her influence for the betterment of others, and in doing so she left behind an amazing legacy and will forever be remembered in history as an inspirational figure. Her life produced many quotes – one that is most pivotal is, 'fight for the things you care about but do it in a way that will lead others to join you'. She will forever be known as the notorious RBG.

As you can see, there are many ways to leave a legacy; some are as a direct result of your actions, others are because of how people remember you. Most people don't think of the legacy that they wish to leave behind, or if they do it may be when they are in the later stages of their lives and are reflecting on the life they have lived so far.

We all have the opportunity to create an amazing legacy, to make a difference and leave the world a better place. It is up to each of us individually if we wish to do so.

Where to from here?

My aim in writing this book was to educate and empower you to think about your legacy, to think about your life and to think about what you want to leave behind for your loved ones and how you would like to be remembered. Many people travel through life and think they lead an insignificant life, you and you alone have the power to determine your legacy and the influence that you have on others while you are alive and also when you are no longer here.

Throughout this book I have attempted to cover the aspects that businesspeople and entrepreneurs constantly tell me are important to them, and I hope that in doing so I have provided some clarity to the questions that you may have had when you started reading this book.

It was my wish to make what can be a difficult topic somewhat more positive. I hope that it gives you the courage to know that armed with the right information and tools you can put in place a fantastic Estate Plan irrespective of what your circumstances are. I hope it encourages you to think deeply about your family, your loved ones and what is important to you. More importantly, I hope it inspires you to put your Estate Plan in place, to leave a wonderful legacy, and to provide you and your family with peace of mind knowing that your estate planning affairs are all in place.

If this book resonates with you or has impacted you, I would love to hear from you and can be contacted at melisa@madisonsloanlawyers.com.au

If you would like to work with me to put in place your Estate Plan, I encourage you to head to our website www.madisonsloanlawyers.com.au or contact me at melisa@madisonsloanlawyers.com.au

About the author

Melisa Sloan is an estate planning and probate lawyer and is the founder of Madison Sloan Lawyers, a Melbourne-based boutique law firm.

Having had the privilege of assisting thousands of clients put in place their estate plans during her legal career, Melisa understands the challenges business owners and entrepreneurs face in considering their legacy and how best to look after their family. She has used this extensive experience to help business owners and entrepreneurs create lasting legacies that ensure their families and loved ones are well cared for and that their business is taken care of if something were to happen to them.

Melisa has witnessed the grief and stress that can be left behind by those that don't take the time to put their estate planning affairs in order and is a strong advocate for educating clients so that they can make informed decisions about how they can best look after their families and loved ones in the most asset-protective and tax-effective manner in the event that they become incapacitated or are no longer here.

As a lawyer, Melisa derives great joy in listening to people's stories, to what is important and what resonates with them, and she acknowledges the enormous privilege she has in being able to make a difference in their life.

Melisa is a daughter, sister, aunt, great aunt, godmother and amazing friend who loves people and is passionate about helping people leave beautiful and inspiring legacies.

Connect with Melisa

Email: melisa@madisonsloanlawyers.com.au
Website: www.madisonsloanlawyers.com.au
Facebook: www.facebook.com/madisonsloanlawyers
Instagram: www.instagram.com/melisa_sloan_

Acknowledgements

There are so many incredible people who travelled this journey with me and helped bring this book to life.

My wonderful parents Terry and Barbara, for always being there for me and having an enormous influence on my life, your constant support is so very much appreciated.

To my family, friends and colleagues thank you for sharing this journey with me, for listening to me share my vision and the countless conversations you so generously had with me throughout this time. Particular mention must go to Maddi, Aimee, Deb, Ange, Michelle and Maria. To my team at Madison Sloan Lawyers thank you for being superstars and putting up with me talking about this book.

To Peta, a big thank you for all your ideas and for coming up with the design concept for this cover. I will forever be grateful to you.

My clients who provided me with the inspiration for writing this book, thank you for so openly sharing your lives and trusting in me, I am so grateful that I get to wake up and do what I love every day and it is an absolute privilege to assist you.

Clarissa Rayward for being so inspirational and supportive in all that you do, and for being the very reason that this book was written. You definitely make my life in law land so much more enjoyable. To the wonderful Authors Inc tribe thank you for always being so encouraging and supportive, each and every one of you are amazing, and to my book buddy Lynda – thank you.

Andrew Griffiths, thank you for all your guidance and support – without you this book may never have been written.